Christian
Mission
in the
Postmodern
World

An Intrusive
Gospel?

C. Norman
Kraus

InterVarsity Press
Downers Grove, Illinois

InterVarsity Press
P.O. Box 1400, Downers Grove, IL 60515
World Wide Web: www.ivpress.com
E-mail: mail@ivpress.com

©*1998 by C. Norman Kraus*

InterVarsity Press® is the book-publishing division of InterVarsity Christian Fellowship/USA®, a student movement active on campus at hundreds of universities, colleges and schools of nursing in the United States of America, and a member movement of the International Fellowship of Evangelical Students. For information about local and regional activities, write Public Relations Dept., InterVarsity Christian Fellowship/USA, 6400 Schroeder Rd., P.O. Box 7895, Madison, WI 53707-7895.

Scripture quotations, unless otherwise noted, are from the New Revised Standard Version of the Bible, copyright 1989 by the Division of Christian Education of the National Council of the Churches of Christ in the USA. Used by permission. All rights reserved.*

ISBN 0-8308-1546-5

Printed in the United States of America ♾

Library of Congress Cataloging-in-Publication Data

Kraus, C. Norman (Clyde Norman), 1924-
  An intrusive Gospel? : Christian witness in a postmodern world /
C. Norman Kraus.
    p. cm.
  Includes bibliographical references.
  ISBN 0-8308-1546-5 (alk. paper)
  1. Missions—Theory. 2. Christianity and culture. 3. Missions—
History—20th century. I. Title.
BV2063.K77 1998
266'.001—dc21   97-46379
                                                                                          CIP

18	17	16	15	14	13	12	11	10	9	8	7	6	5	4	3	2	1
13	12	11	10	09	08	07	06	05	04	03	02	01	00	99	98		

To Earl and Pat Hostetter Martin,
servants of Christ

Preface —————————————————————— 7

Introduction ————————————————————— 9

1 Christian Witness in a Postmodern Context ————— 17

2 Intervention: Presence & Proclamation ——————— 39

3 Reorienting the Conceptual Framework for Mission —— 51

4 What Kind of Intervention? Defining the "Spiritual" —— 63

5 A Christian Spirituality for Intervention Ministries —— 77

6 Conversion & Social Transformation:

   "Engaging the Powers" ———————————————— 93

7 Relating to People of Other Faiths ————————— 111

Notes ————————————————————————— 133

For Further Reading ——————————————————— 139

Preface

These chapters were begun as a series of lecture-discussions with the staff of the Mennonite Central Committee, the united relief and social service agency of Mennonite and Brethren in Christ churches, in the spring of 1994. While these reflections were originally written in the context of a "service agency," it is my conviction that, except for tactical reasons on certain occasions, the evangelism-service dichotomy should be dropped. The larger strategy of Christian mission should combine the two into a dynamic whole. Thus I hope my essay can furnish theological insight that will profit both missions and service agency personnel, as well as any readers who have questions about the appropriateness of any kind of cultural intervention.

I owe a special word of thanks to John A. Lapp, at that time the executive secretary of MCC, and to Judy Zimmerman Herr and David Schrock Shenk for their continued support and helpful criticism. Paul Gingrich, of the Mennonite Board of Missions, read an early version and gave helpful suggestions. Others from Eastern Mennonite University, including Vernon Jantzi, Wayne Teel, Calvin Shenk and Myron Augsburger, have read all or parts of the manuscript in process.

Finally, I owe a special word of thanks to Donald Kraybill and the Young Center Program of Elizabethtown College, under whose auspices I prepared and gave the original lectures for the Mennonite Central Committee staff. The Center's invitation to be a Young Center Fellow in the spring of 1994 prompted me to initiate the project, and the Center supported me through its initial stages.

Introduction

When I used the word *intervention* in the title of my original lectures, I thought I noticed a few raised eyebrows. These indicated more surprise than disapproval. Less militant words like *presence* and *dialogue* seemed more in tune with the present mood of crosscultural work. But I would argue that observation, presence, dialogue and the like are also kinds of intervention, and that the issue is what kind of intervention is valid and valuable. The incarnation of God in Christ was an intervention—indeed, a most extraordinary and incredible one.

Growing disillusionment with growth-oriented "Third World" economic development in the 1970s and 1980s and increasing awareness of what Walter Wink calls the "domination" factor that has been implicit in Western Christendom's missionary ventures have raised red flags about the validity and value of cultural intervention. Boards review priorities and strategies. Field personnel search for a rationale and strategies to justify their presence, and potential service and missionary personnel have begun to wonder whether their anticipated assignments may not be presumptuous intrusions.

Beyond Domination
Cultural aggression and domination have been a problem for

both religious and secular crosscultural missions. It is true
that the church felt fully justified in an aggressive "spiritual"
intervention which it did not recognize as cultural intrusion.
Even so, it can be plausibly argued that religious missions
have on the whole been far more sensitive to the values of
local culture than secular economic and military missions
that disclaimed any cultural religious meddling. For example, William Carey clearly attempted to respect Bengali
culture and change it from within, through the creation of a
modern Bengali prose and the translation of both the Bible
and Hindu classics into the modernized language. Unfortunately, too many other missionaries failed to exhibit this
same sensitivity.

We must confess that religious missions have been too
closely allied with and dependent on the secular goals and
military power of intervening national agencies. They envisioned the Christian mission moving forward "like a mighty
army," and they were too often characterized by the same
colonial style as their secular counterparts. As Western
churches have become more aware of the valid insights of
cultural anthropology, they have begun to question their
previous tendency to identify Western civilization and modernization with the gospel message and its cultural impact.
They have become far more aware of the difference between
evangelization and proselytization. Now the rubrics are
"proclamation," "indigenization," "contextualization," "dialogue," "mutuality," "appropriate technology" and the like.

Both service agencies and mission boards have wrestled
with the problems of Western domination on mission fields
and have sought better strategies for holistic mission. Obviously the actual work of evangelical mission boards has not
been limited to the strictly "spiritual" aspects of human life.
From the beginning they have engaged in educational, relief

and other "social services" projects. But they have attempted to contain their work under the rubric of evangelism and church planting, and they have been slow to acknowledge that the contribution of social services to their mission is "spiritual." At best they have recognized it as "pre-evangelism."

In evangelical Protestant circles, Christian aid organizations usually have been recognized as "parachurch"—that is, having a church connection of some kind but not an essential organizational connection to denominational structures. For pragmatic reasons, if no other, evangelical service agencies have accepted this division of mission responsibilities. Roman Catholics have been more accepting and inclusive in their classification.

Even evangelical denominations, like the Mennonites, that have organized both mission boards and service agencies have assumed the traditional dualistic distinction between the spiritual and the physical-social and have structured their agencies accordingly. In spite of an increasing use of the term *holistic* to describe their intentions, the search for a holistic approach to intervention ministries has been painfully slow and tortuous. It has been deemed politic to organize congruent with the evangelical dictum "evangelism *and* social service." Mission boards sponsor evangelization and "church planting," while service agencies do "Christian" emergency relief and service work but are not expected to plant churches.

This bifurcation of roles has been accentuated by service workers hesitant to impose Western analyses and service programs on those they have gone to help. They hesitate to impose a "Western gospel" on Asian and African cultures. Often they accept assignments to work in local church programs, and they leave evangelism to the locals in order to avoid triumphalist evangelism. At the same time, mission agencies have tended to restrict "mission" to church planting and thus have been tempted to minimize the contributions of service personnel to church planting.

Increasingly it has become clear that this is both a pragmatic and a theological blunder. Organizationally, lines need to be redrawn. Instead of pursuing a "two-track" strategy, we need to begin thinking in terms of two rails on the same track. Or perhaps we could use the metaphor of the Amazon River with its many tributaries. These tributaries bring their various silts and colors to mingle in the one Amazon, the lifeline of Brazil.

Beyond Greek Dualism

Biblical understandings of the holistic nature of human beings "in the image of God" must be recovered. The psychosomatic essence of human beings must be defined to include both social and spiritual dimensions. The traditional Greek dualism between spirit and body, which has informed and often distorted Western theology, must be more thoroughly purged without simply reducing the "spirit" to cortical activity of the brain!

We need to move beyond the notion of "humanitarian" service and "spiritual" salvation as discrete, definable activities. Christ's words "Just as you did it to one of the least of these . . . you did it to me" (Mt 25:40) imply the genuinely spiritual character of agapaic[1] social and material services "in the name of Christ." Such service is a necessary component of Christian witness to the gospel. We need to rediscover the integrated meaning of biblical shalom as the mission of the church in both theory and practice.

Already in the second century of our era the Gnostic heresies, influenced by Neo-Platonic philosophy, spoke of the body-soul on the one hand and the spirit on the other as though they were two distinct beings. They held that these two distinct essences are individual beings that combine to make up the human being. The soul, or reason, was associated with the life of the body, which is destined to die. Only the spirit is eternal and capable of ultimate salvation. Salvation of the spirit is to be attained through spiritual knowledge *(gnōsis)* of God, the Ultimate Principle. Thus life in this world counts for little except as it enables one to discover the inner mystery of God. This fateful schism in the understanding of humanness has continued to plague Christian theology through the ages, and it now has a champion in popular fundamentalism. It is graphically illustrated by Dwight L. Moody's evaluation of social work as "polishing the brass on a sinking ship."

Evangelical Protestant theology rather too easily accepted the secularist identification of the psychosomatic with empirical physical existence, and then defined the spirit in gnostic fashion as an added theological endowment. In so doing it has tended to ignore the essentially spiritual character of the psychosomatic, or body-soul, dimensions of human nature.

At best the spiritual and physical have been treated as two poles of a continuum, but a continuum that has been seriously disrupted by original sin. Since renewal of the spirit is viewed as a purely supernatural intervention, the continuum of human social services and spiritual salvation is rejected. Thus in evangelical missiology *holistic* can mean only a proper symmetry between the two separate and distinct factors of our dualistic existence—body and spirit—which translates into a strategy of "evangelism *and* social service."

The problem is exacerbated by the exclusive association

of *social* with collective physical existence and *spiritual* with an individual "personal" essence. *Social,* in this way of thinking, refers to an empirical inclination and activity of rational animals, while *spiritual* refers to the personal essence of individuals. Salvation means that the individual spirit is reunited with the divine Spirit by a spiritual rebirth. The social dimension of reunion with one's fellow human beings is entirely secondary and derivative from the spiritual rebirth.

In such a formula, *holistic* means treating the psycho-physical and the spiritual in a properly balanced fashion, which, of course, assumes that the spiritual has exclusive priority. (One is reminded of the contests between the medieval popes and emperors who argued over the priority of temporal or spiritual authority!) Individual, personal salvation of the soul, or spirit, is separated from and given priority over relief and "social service," which are reduced to a "humanistic" activity.

An Overview

The following chapters are an attempt to redraw the lines between the spiritual and social-physical dimensions of life. *Spirit* or *spiritual* as applied to human beings is spoken of in Scripture as "the image of God." Human beings in their physical-psychical-social being are spiritual, that is, made in the image of God. In Scripture the spirit is not envisioned as a separate part of one's individual being. Rather, spirit is that dimension of our being in which we as psychosomatic social creatures are related to God.

Because we are spiritual beings, we find our self-identity in a transcendent dimension. All the other dimensions of our life are caught up in and given meaning by the Transcendent Reality in whom we "live and move and have our being"

(Acts 17:28). Our salvation is attained in recognizing and participating in the true nature of this Transcendence. The degree of our participation in the reality of God's rule is the measure of our spirituality. Christianity claims that Jesus is the true and living way to this "beatitude"—this blessed identification of ourselves as responsible children in the family of God. This essay explores the implications of this basic truth for the holistic mission of the church.

In the first chapter we look at the change in cultural assumptions that underlay the old aggressive, even imperialistic approach to evangelism and missions to traditional cultures. This change is sometimes called a "paradigm shift" because it is profound enough to have marked the end of an old era and the beginning of a new one. It is often referred to as a shift from "modern" to "postmodern" thinking. The old rationalistic assumption that we in the Western world have superior knowledge (*gnōsis*/truth) which others must accept on our terms in order to be "saved" has been challenged by a new cultural relativism. For Christians this cultural relativism suggests that all our human knowledge is relative to *God's* truth, and God's truth can be found only through our attempts to live it out in whatever culture we find ourselves. "Living it out" across cultures requires us to enter deeply into each others' lives, sharing experience and receiving as well as giving.

Such a change in understanding has significant implications for the church's mission in the world. In the chapters following we explore these implications. What kind of intervention is appropriate to the essential message of the gospel? What is the goal of such intervention? In theological terms, we sometimes speak of the change required by the gospel as a "spiritual conversion." What does it mean to speak of humankind as "spiritual" beings? And what does "spiritual" conversion entail? Is it related at all to social transformation? If so, how?

The culture in which the Bible was written was very different from ours in its presuppositions and definitions. Yet if we can open ourselves to its cultural perspectives, we may be surprised by the new light that it throws on our postmodern situation.

1

Christian Witness in a Postmodern Context

●●

*F*EW OF US ARE AWARE OF HOW PROFOUNDLY THE PROCESS of modernization has affected both our theology and our concept of the Christian mission in the world. This is true for conservative as well as liberal Christians. The great missionary movement of the nineteenth and early twentieth centuries, of which the church's service programs are a vital part, was the historical counterpart of Western modernization, and the gospel we have preached from our position of power has contained more promise of upward mobility through technology and democracy than we may have intended.

Now social analysts are talking about a cultural paradigm shift, and they refer to our present era as "postmodern" and "post-Christian." This shift can be compared to the shift from the Ptolemaic to the Copernican view of the universe, which introduced the "modern" period. Now in the place of universal laws of nature that operate with objective, rational precision, we think in terms of Einstein's theory of relativity and a more subjective, personal theory of knowledge and communication. This involves changes in the way we perceive reality and the way we understand language, meaning and truth.

Some of the resultant changes, such as those introduced by new computer technologies, are obvious. But there are other, more subtle changes in the way we think about our world that have just as radically affected us. New perspectives on language and culture have resulted in new insights into the communication process. New perceptions of how the biblical text is related to its premodern Near Eastern cultural context have clearly changed our interpretative and communicative modes. Changes in our attitudes toward racial and ethnic differences, changes in our cultural and moral values, greater openness to the validity of intuitive awareness and less certainty about "scientific" reality—all these and many other changes have transformed our way of thinking.

This paradigm shift is also described as a disavowal of the eighteenth- and nineteenth-century Enlightenment mentality that assumed the superiority of Western culture and its right to dominate the rest of the world because it was rational and scientific. By the same token it assumed the superiority of cultural Christianity and the need to re-create the "heathen" world in its own image. The postmodern era into which we are entering is characterized by a chastened confidence in objective human reason, technology and the inevitability of human progress. And accordingly, the postmodern Christian mood is far less imperialistic.

The radical shift in intellectual, cultural and political patterns unavoidably affects the meaning of "Christian" presence in the world. Whether we recognize it or not, it affects both the concept and the outcomes of the church's mission. Since the meaning of our actions is conditioned by the cultural context, there is no escaping. Whether we change the external patterns or not, the inner meaning of our actions is changed.

By implication, postmodern presuppositions challenge traditional evangelism as cultural arrogance. They throw suspicion on a service motivation as disguised self-serving. And they suggest that development through modernization is simply a new imperialism. Thus whether we agree with these postmodern implications or not, they demand a change in attitudes, modes of communication and definitions of witness and service. I suspect that in part our uneasiness, our self-searching and our experimentation in service and witness programs have grown out of our uncertainty about how to respond to this paradigm change.

Our gradual adaptation to these changes in thought patterns, values and attitudes add up to a change in worldview. Our philosophies of life have subtly changed, even though we have maintained much of our older vocabulary. For this reason it seems necessary to begin this essay with a theological analysis of the paradigm shift itself as it affects the church's mission in the world. Then in the following chapters we will explore some of the effects from a Christian theological perspective.

Effects of the Paradigm Shift

First, then, let me briefly characterize the underlying changes from the modern to the postmodern outlook as they affect our mission. Of course the postmodern perspective does not negate or contradict the modern at every point. Indeed, in some sense it grows out of a radical application of the empirical, or scientific, methodology. Nevertheless, it does present us with a striking shift in cultural perceptions.

The modern era has been dominated by the "scientific" worldview and methodology. It began with an assumption that the knower and the known are distinctly separate objects. The objective viewer gathers knowledge of the "facts" by controlled observation and experimentation. The less subjective the involvement of the researcher with the object of investigation, the better—the purer the objective knowledge obtained. This led to a definition of truth as fact. Truth, according to this view, is a rational, scientifically based conclusion. All other, nonempirically based claims were classed as "opinions," and where opinions were the result of illogical, unexamined attitudes, they were called "superstition."

Working with this definition of truth, fundamentalist Protestants defined revelation as such objective, rational, factual data. They accepted the empirical, or scientific, idea of truth as fact, but they rejected the notion that the scientific method is the only way to establish factual truth. One illustration will suffice. The contemporary debate over evolution turns on these definitions. Fundamentalists hold that the supernatural revelation of the Bible establishes the scientific "truth" of creationism. The Bible's "truth" is fact based on supernatural disclosure rather than scientific discovery. And all other opinion that is not based on either empirical documentation or revelation is superstition.

Now it will be obvious that when "prescientific" and nonbiblical cultures are evaluated from the perspectives of such a paradigm, they will be judged negatively. The common descriptive categories, such as "primitive," "undeveloped" or at least "underdeveloped," "traditional," "superstitious" and "heathen darkness," confirm the point. The purpose of intervention is defined as modernization, development, scientific education, evangelism and conversion to the "objective" truth. And no matter how empathic and compassionate the change agents might be, they become power brokers and are cast into the role of "benefactors" and patrons (Lk 22:25-27).

The goal of the rational process, called modernization, is the independence—self-sufficiency and self-determination—of individuals. The aim of modernization is to free individuals from fatalism and traditional communalism. Thus those who possess rational truth have the "right" to intervene, and their rational purpose gives them the "right" to dominate the nonliterate, the undeveloped, the traditional and superstitious. They exert this right for the good of individuals bound in irrational superstition.

Remember that we are not necessarily describing a conscious thought process or organizational rationale. We are uncovering the subconscious thought patterns, presuppositions and cultural assumptions—the paradigm—that shape the ends and means of our intervention projects. And this paradigm has controlled both conservative and liberal rationalists.[1]

Finally, the modernist paradigm has been dominated by an overweening optimism. Progress through rational manipulation has been considered inevitable. Both rationally and technologically, the superiority of modernism is considered self-evident! It is assumed that the laws of reason control the economic sphere, if not the political. They were even read into the evolutionary process in social Darwinism.

While the doctrine of inevitable evolutionary progress was rejected by most religious missions, they had their own adaptations of the concept. Earlier mainline theologians pictured the eschatological future in terms of a triumphal church moving toward a victorious conclusion of this age under the leadership of Christ and the Spirit. This was known as postmillennialism. But even the more pessimistic premillennialists moved confidently ahead. Assured that they had the absolute (rational) "truth," they prayed for the end of the age, when Jesus would return to vindicate them and rule with a rod of iron over the forces of darkness. They were the shock troops for what in the final outcome would be victory for God and the truth of revelation.

The emerging postmodern paradigm has challenged this imperialistic approach of the modern West to traditional cultures. Here I cannot enter the major debate that is raging around the term *postmodern*. Each analyst has his or her own definition.[2] But let us note several fundamental changes in perspective that affect our approach to cultural intervention.

First, "knowing" is understood to be participatory activity, which gives all knowledge a degree of subjectivity. Already thirty years ago Michael Polanyi, a philosopher of science, was pointing out that the scientific process is not nearly as objective as rational empiricism assumed. Scientists belong to a community of thought with its presuppositions, which influence their resultant knowledge. Further, it had been pointed out earlier that their measurements actually cause changes in the data measured. Sociologists began to talk about a "sociology of knowledge," pointing out that how we define truth is in part determined by subjective factors of our cultural environment. In some sense, then, "truth is relative to the community of knowers,"[3] and all our knowledge is incomplete.

This strongly suggests that the pursuit of knowledge is a shared quest. One cannot assume that one has absolute, objective knowledge which is then simply to be transmitted to the ignorant. The pursuit of knowledge must be dialogical. An illustration from scientific medicine helps to elucidate this point. The past fifty years have seen a marked change of attitude and perspective in medical research. No longer are traditional cures simply written off as nonscientific. While they are not accepted uncritically, they are examined in a respectful dialogue with the local culture in which they are found.

But the question remains whether this has any direct bearing on the knowledge we have by revelation. Is not revelation an absolute, objective transmission of divine data that transcends all cultural change and relativity? As a matter of fact, the central conviction of Christian faith, namely, incarnation, belies this notion of truth.

The Word of God became flesh and blood and lived among us in a culturally conditioned existence. Jesus himself insisted that knowledge of God comes through personal participation and response to his covenant purposes for the human family (Jn 8:31-32). And while we do not doubt the transcendent reality of God and the truth of his Word, we know that our own knowledge of that truth is relational and relative. We "get to know" God through a living, dialogical relationship with others as we attempt to do his will. Thus we approach others, who are also "in the image of God," in a dialogical, not a monological, mode.[4] We will pursue this further in the final chapter on our approach to other religions.

Two final facets of postmodernism which change the perspective on intervention need yet to be noted. First, being itself is understood as a kind of relation, not as an unchanging substance. To be is to be part of and participate in the whole web of existence. Thus, by definition, being involves interdependence and process. It involves doing and relating. This challenges modernization's concept of individualism and independence as the final value and suggests community (shalom) as the goal of our intervention.

Last, the postmodernist perspective challenges the idea of

inevitable progress. It views change in a much more realistic and relational manner. It takes seriously the implications of Werner Heisenberg's uncertainty principle for history in general. Change is the product of undetermined organic and historical interaction. The notion that Enlightenment rationalism has discovered and co-opted the laws of inevitable evolutionary progress is seriously doubted. The postmodernist outlook is more realistic about the unmitigated superiority of Western science and much less confident that modernization is the answer for traditional cultures.

New Understandings of Cultural Dynamics

The paradigm shift that I have just described has influenced our understanding of the communication process and the relativity of human values. It has made us more aware of how the meaning of our actions and words is related to cultural change. And it has reminded us once again of our cultural interdependence and the relativity of our cultural existence. We are indeed creatures of time and space, caught up in a web of changing humanity. New insights into the nature of cultures, therefore, are important for the formation of outcomes and strategy of our intervention ministries. Cultural anthropologists have, in fact, made many observations about cultural change which have a direct bearing on our approach.

First, we have learned that all cultures are dynamic and constantly changing. Even so-called traditional cultures change and adapt to new situations. This in itself is an important insight. Earlier in the twentieth century, anthropologists described cultures as static and even suggested that it was inappropriate for missionaries to try to change them. Now I think we understand that cultural change is inevitable, even though it may not always be desirable. The forces of modernization are irrevocable, and we must wrestle with the question of *appropriate* change.

We have become much more sophisticated about the nature and effects of change. We have learned that "primitive" does not necessarily mean retarded or undeveloped. Neither does modernization necessarily result in authentic human development. The modern emphasis on individualism can lead to narcissism and anarchy. Modern technology can destroy the social web and threaten the ecological balance. Our task is to work creatively with respect for the integrity of host cultures to bring about those changes that promote authentic human community under God. Our model as Christians is biblical *shalom* (peace), modeled after Jesus' pattern of the kingdom of God.

Second, we have learned that all cultures, including Christian culture, are relative to the biblical ideal of the kingdom of God. Indeed, there are many conflicting cultural expressions within Christianity itself. Cultural Christianity of the West is not a revealed religious expression to be identified with the kingdom of God. While Protestants long ago rejected the infallibility of one catholic, or ecumenical, church, the idea that Christian culture is the revealed norm for all cultures dies hard.

The older missionary assumption was that Western culture is the normative expression of biblical revelation and that traditional non-Western cultures should be brought into line with the culture of Christendom. The goal was to produce duplicate societies and churches. This was graphically illustrated in the film *The Mission.* The Spanish Jesuits tried to build a replica of Catholic piety in the Brazilian rain forests, only to have it destroyed by Portuguese Christian soldiers. While this assumption that the church and the kingdom of God are identical was at its height in the Middle

Ages, it has died a very slow death.

The other side of this coin is that there are cultures outside the biblical tradition which have the potential to be viable expressions of the gospel. Variations in cultural religious expressions in our world exist on a relative scale. There may be human and religious values in cultures outside the historical biblical tradition that excel those of our own Western expressions. For example, we appreciate the Inuit spiritual sensitivity to nature, the Coptic respect for dignity and form in worship, the Islamic reverence for divine covenant law, the Buddhist regard for the wholeness of the cosmic order of which the individual is simply a part, and the traditional African respect for family continuity through the generations.

Third, the biblical culture and message cannot be equated with Western Christian expressions of them, whether orthodox or liberal. The theoretical recognition of this is as old as the Reformation, which drew a sharp line between church tradition and the Bible. However, we have been slow to recognize the ramifications of this "Protestant principle." Our constant tendency has been to equate our Protestant orthodoxies with "The Bible says . . . !" As recent as the 1980s a missionary scholar in Japan insisted that Christianity's initial movement westward instead of eastward was a special leading of the Spirit that worked to preserve the purity of the biblical message. He virtually equated conservative Protestantism of the nineteenth century with the biblical norm.

This presumption is very old and very stubborn. In fact, it was built into the definition of "orthodoxy" in the ecumenical creeds of the third and fourth centuries. Orthodoxy was defined as what has been believed in the church always and everywhere. That implies that the philosophical language of the creeds, which in fact represents three centuries of development and a radically different cultural setting, is an exact replication of the biblical message. Thus began the substitution of the authority of church tradition for the original biblical message.

Especially in cultures where the pace of change is relatively slow, it is difficult to understand that historical change results in distinct cultural mutations which in turn affect the essential meaning of language and life. In cases of more rapid change it is more easily perceived. For example, the changes that have taken place in Japanese culture over the past fifty years are so drastic that it is difficult for contemporary Japanese readers to understand the pre-World War II meaning of words that are still in common use. The simple expression of thanks "Arigatoo gozaimasu" literally means "It is a hard thing [you place on me]" and formerly expressed the burden of responsibility that a gift conveys. It did not express the Western meaning of delight and appreciation.

Take another very current example. Although Thomas Jefferson's America was quite different from the contemporary culture of Virginia and Washington, D.C., American politicians continue to justify current political action by appealing to his literal words. And conservative pundits continue to appeal to nineteenth-century America to justify late twentieth-century social and political policy. In similar fashion, religious conservatives continue to identify the biblical message with their current orthodoxies and have tried to enforce uniform and universal interpretations.

This leads to a fourth observation concerning the important and in fact inescapable necessity of contextualizing the biblical message. To contextualize means to adapt the words and actions used to express the gospel to a cultural context. It is a kind of translation. The purpose is to allow the original meaning of the message to be expressed in understandable terms. Contextualization will include not only verbal adaptations and ideas but also style of intervention and the priority given to action and words.

Throughout the centuries the church has contextualized the cultural expression of biblical meaning and values. In earlier centuries the process was unstudied and natural. For the literate populace, the gospel message was put into the constructs of Greek philosophy. For the preliterate, religious art visualized the Bible stories in the contemporary context. For example, biblical soldiers were depicted wearing the armor of the artist's time and nation. Buildings, landscapes, facial features and style of clothing of the artist's time and place provided the visual image of the story and gave its meaning a distinct coloration.

Today we dare not be naive about this process of contextualization. In the words of Paul Hiebert, we must be "critical."[5] That is, we must be deliberate and analytical as we approach the communicative process. We must also recognize that the resultant contextualized picture cannot be substituted for the original biblical picture as we cross cultures. Until very recently we simply did not recognize the importance of this point for conveying the gospel across cultures.

Fifth, we are beginning to realize how crucial is the tie between relationship, communication and truth. Communication of truth is impossible apart from mutually respectful and deferential relationship. In many cultures, such as those of Asia, truth in relationship is more important than ideational truth.

The New Testament's insistence that we should consider others more significant than ourselves is not a matter of pious self-depreciation. It is a necessary stance for effective communication of the truth about Jesus. For example, how can our Muslim brothers and sisters understand the profound truth of God's vulnerability in the incarnation if we relate to them as invulnerable, superior persons and insist that their cultural patterns must yield to ours? Paul calls the "gospel" of God's gracious relation to us "the word of the truth" (Col 1:5). A proper relationship to God and to each other is the "truth [as it] is in Jesus" (Eph 4:21). Authentic human relationship creates the possibility of communication, and truth is the shape of authentic communication.

Mapping the Communication Process
More than thirty years ago, Eugene Nida called for a distinct paradigm shift in the crosscultural communication of the gospel. In his *Message and Mission* (1960) he called it a shift from the "two language" model to the "three language" model for communication. The implications of this shift have finally caught up with us, and we are only now seriously wrestling with them. Figure 1 diagrams the traditional two-

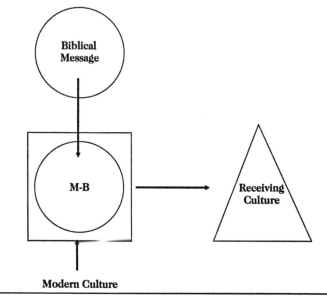

Figure 1. Traditional evangelical linguistic model

language model, and figure 2 diagrams the three-language model.

The traditional two-language model assumes that the original biblical message *(B)* is identical with the modern Western evangelical contextualization *(M)* of it. Thus the task is to simply transmit across cultures the modern cultural orthodoxy. The transmission process is by definition "monological"—that is, truth is spoken to ignorance and untruth. As we have seen, this assumes the Enlightenment concept of truth as a rational idea, and this model has dominated both our evangelistic and our service interventions. The solid arrow-line from the sending culture to the receiving culture illustrates this relationship.

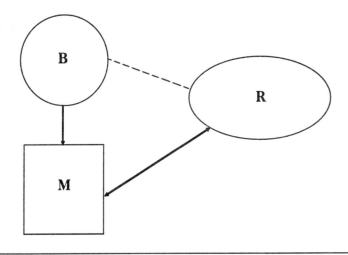

Figure 2. Three-language model

The three-language model indicates a much more radical change than the simple diagram might suggest. It begins with the assumption that the biblical message was given in a cultural context and form different from our modern culture. The biblical message informs our modern expression of the gospel but is not identical with it. (The vertical solid arrow-line from *B* to *M* indicates this.)

Second, use of an elliptical shape to diagram the receiving culture suggests that it may be closer to the biblical context than the modern sending culture. For example, the Luo culture of East Africa has retained a procedure for reconciling an offender with a blood sacrifice.[6] This sets up the possibility that our modern missioners should be open to new perspectives and meanings from Scripture as they learn from other cultures. It implies the need for dialogical interaction in communicating the message of Christ.

Third, the dotted line between *B* and *R* indicates the need to set up a direct interaction between the original biblical context and the receiving culture. This insight has changed the way in which translation of the Bible into tribal languages is being done. In the case of Indian tribes of the Argentine Chaco, a North American translator who knew English, Spanish and Greek worked with a local tribesperson who knew Spanish and Toba. The Western translator engaged the native linguist in an intimate, dialogical process as they together attempted a "critical contextualization" of the biblical message.

In the case of service workers, the way the Bible is studied in "base communities" provides an example of direct involvement in interpreting and applying Scripture. Here the Scriptures are read together in the local language and applied according to the insights of the group.

In a more formal way I have described this new model in *The Authentic Witness* as follows:

Our contemporary witness (or translation) of the biblical message cannot be equated with the biblical witness itself. It is at best a cultural translation interposed between the original and the new culture to which it is being presented. Thus there is at least a three-way dissimilarity between the participants. Nor can we assume that our own secular western culture is nearer to the Bible than are the cultures to which it is being introduced. When we recognize that some of the cultures receiving the gospel may in fact be nearer to the biblical culture than that of the missionary, it becomes apparent that the spirit of dialogue is fundamental to authentic witness. Indeed, missionaries from the West may receive much new understanding. This is what Fred Smith has called "the mutuality of evangelism."[7]

With minimal adaptation we could use figures 1 and 2 to plot the characteristics of modern and postmodern approaches to crosscultural mission (both service and proclamation ministries). In the modern era, the donor/agent has assumed the right to control and manage the funds and activities. Both development and evangelism models have assumed this mode. Lines of definition and authority flow one way.

Perhaps the most significant change indicated by the emerging postmodern perspective is the need to change this one-way planning and management approach. We must continue to shift the emphasis to "sharing," "witness," "presence," "dialogue" and "contextualization."

This indicates a much more appreciative attitude toward the receptor cultures and an attempt to involve them in their own change process. While the Christ of Scripture remains normative, recognition of the relativities of our own culture and the possibilities of other cultures to receive and express the gospel need to be recognized. This will require a deliberate effort to strengthen the relationship between the biblical culture and the traditional cultures of the so-called Third, Fourth and Fifth worlds which have received Western missions.

Theological Perspectives on the Postmodern Situation
The postmodern religious perspective is inherently plural-

istic and relativistic. As such, it challenges the validity of Christian intervention with an explicit goal to expedite cultural and religious change.[8] It celebrates diversity and relativity and advocates a dialogical search for solutions to human problems. Such a perspective has definite implications for an approach to social development. Some of these offer a corrective to past theory and practice. Some even highlight biblical principles that we have overlooked in the past. At the same time, the implications of its inherent relativism threaten the very foundations of the Christian missions and development enterprise as we have known it. Thus we need a theological as well as pragmatic analysis and critique of these implications insofar as they affect that mission.

We need to reevaluate Western culture in both its conservative and liberal guises. Western culture has by no means been an unmixed blessing! Individualism within fundamentalism has been as harmful as liberal individualism. The same can be said of the spirit of confrontive superiority so evident already in the linking of "civilizing" with "converting." I am not referring to the intolerance of individual missioners but to the cultural presuppositions that have permeated and shaped our intercultural approaches.

A theological perspective will not give us tactical answers, but it can help us to set priorities, strategy and goals. Comparisons of theological beliefs and attitudes toward development strategies and goals indicate that there is a clear correlation between the two. For example, a study by Merrill Ewert and associates at Cornell University shows that people holding to traditional Protestant belief patterns tend to favor "assistance-based approaches" to development over "facilitative approaches."[9] With that in mind, I want to close this chapter with a few theological observations that have a bearing on our approach to development ministries.

Our first reaction to the postmodern paradigm shift is likely to be apprehension. If one accepts the new definitions and assumptions, can development projects any longer be viewed as "gospel"? Must we take the word *evangelical* (from the Greek *euangelion,* meaning good news) out of our development vocabulary? Can we continue to think of development as a Christian mission and speak specifically of Christian goals for development?

Of course if we begin with a thoroughly relativistic assumption such as the deconstructionists follow, we cannot logically maintain our claim of universal validity for the truth that is in Jesus. However, such radical relativism has its own set of logical difficulties, which we cannot debate here. But if we consider the postmodern protest as a corrective to an overweening rationalism, we can view it as a purgative for modernistic assumptions and attitudes that have crept into nineteenth- and twentieth-century evangelicalism. And inasmuch as the rationalistic spirit, which has for too long dominated orthodox theology, is foreign to the Bible, the postmodern perspective opens up the possibility for new insights into an authentic biblical approach to holistic mission.

This emerging vision sees truth as a way of life in Christ and not as a rational idea, witness as sharing an evangelical life rather than preaching evangelical doctrine, and the end of holistic salvation (shalom) as a shared life in community, not the rescue of individual souls from a sinful social order. (I have stated these couplets in adversarial terms in order to clearly indicate the movement. They are not entirely contradictory, of course.)

In a paper read at a conference to commemorate the seventy-fifth anniversary of the Mennonite Central Committee, Paul Hiebert and his daughter Barbara Hiebert-Crape spoke of the Christian goals of development in this biblical mode. "Our goal in development as Christians," they said, "is to strive towards God's perfect intentions when he created humans. This begins with their full humanity as beings created in the image of God. It finds its full expression in the reconciliation between humans and God, and among one another, that leads to communities of righteousness, peace, love, and harmony with creation, and to the reign of God."[10] One might very well offer this as a biblical view of salvation!

Relativistic pluralism is a typically modern Western option—a carryover of post-Enlightenment thinking. It is the religious parallel to secular political toleration and ultimately can take us only toward secularism. However, it does challenge us to reevaluate our stance toward other cultures and religions that confront us. While I am referring mainly to religions other than Christianity, we must also reposition ourselves vis-à-vis the various orthodoxies of the worldwide church. Christianity has become quite literally a universal religion, but its cultural expressions differ widely, and Christians in development projects need to be related to the local churches.

In all of this *we must distinguish quite clearly between gospel and modernization*. For the first time in two hundred years, modernization is not necessarily linked with Western Christian values. In Japan the disassociation of the two began back in the nineteenth century, and it is now pretty well established in the countries of the Asian rim. For the first time in over two hundred years, the gospel message comes in "weakness" to cultures like Taiwan, Hong Kong and Japan. It comes without the implicit promise of upward social and economic mobility through the altruism of a rich and powerful church and techniques of modernization and entrepreneurial know-how!

What does this "weakness" imply for mission strategy in general? Words that have been used in the Anabaptist tradition to describe this stance of weakness are *servanthood* and *nonviolence.* However, as John Driver points out, "we should not confuse this servanthood with service." He writes:

> Service tends to mean that which is done in the interests of a noble and just cause for which one is struggling. In reality, this may represent a theocratic orientation [domination] even though the means may be nonviolent. Servanthood is symbolized in the church by the basin and the towel and really amounts to a *form of being* more than a *strategy for doing.* Servanthood is the form that the community's concern for persons takes.[11]

Such weakness does not rule out the possibility of material self-improvement for individuals and groups. Nor does it mean that we must revert to a "spiritual" gospel that does not address the socioeconomic aspects of life. However, it also does not promote the superiority of modern civilization or promise the blessings of a consumer society. Servanthood offers a holistic alternative (justice) that does not appeal to economic and military power structures for its sanctions. From the perspectives of power this is "foolishness" and "weakness."

The gospel offers liberation from poverty of spirit, from the greed and fear that impoverish our relationships with others. It offers new motivation and enabling and calls us to "bear one another's burdens" (Gal 6:2). It calls on the privileged to share their advantage—a call that has significant implications for those who go as "servants." It promises a rich life rather than riches in life.

It is important that our service programs be of such a character and spirit that they do not perpetuate the gospel of Christ as the gospel of upward mobility. On the one hand, we must be careful in our service projects not to practice a kind of favoritism toward those who convert to Christianity. Such favoritism has given rise to the epithet "rice Christians." On the other hand, the church as the open community of invitation and servanthood must demonstrate the new possibility of the kingdom of God. As in the first Christian communities, "the name of Jesus" becomes the cohesive and enabling dynamic of a new way of life.

Finally, in light of the impact of secularism we need to quite consciously identify our approach as religious and Christian. Secularism destroys the religious base of premodern cultures in order to save them! Secular development models assume that modernization will be the salvation of traditional societies. We must reject such an assumption. We are not interested in eroding the religious base of premodern societies. Rather, we wish to offer an effective, transforming spiritual alternative that can provide a religious rationale for authentic human development in a modern world.

Thus we need to take the traditional religions seriously, engaging them in respectful dialogue and cooperating with them where possible. Such a serious engagement will require a clear Christian self-identity and discernment within the Christian group. The gospel of the kingdom of God that offers a religious alternative to both secularism and the status quo of traditional religions can furnish discriminating guidance in the selection of postmodern options.

2

Intervention

Presence &
Proclamation

●●

A GREAT DEAL HAS BEEN WRITTEN ABOUT "PRESENCE" IN
contrast to proclamation or evangelization in the mission of
the church, but too often the discussion has been clouded
by the way in which the words are used. Characteristics like
compassion, empathy, respect, humility, openness and *dialogue* are often associated with "presence." Words like *pity,
monologue, arrogance, exclusivism* and *intrusion* are associated with evangelization or proclamation.

Many of the same words associated with "proclamation"
would also be associated with "intervention." Intervention,
it is assumed, implies imposition, patronization and cultural
arrogance that results in ignorance and presumption, however well-intentioned. In reaction to this negative association and frustration with well-intentioned "development"
schemes, there is hesitation to define the church's voluntary
service organizations as institutions for intervention, much

less as change agents. We do not want to be identified as Western agents of cultural change. Service must be low-key—being a "presence," "standing alongside," "suffering with," "identifying with" and "learning from."

Regrettably, we must confess that much evangelism and missionary aid has been culturally insensitive and that many of our best-intentioned efforts have resulted in unintended, though in hindsight quite predictable, negative cultural consequences. Indeed, the gospel itself has been compromised by our cultural presumptions and theological dogmatism. But does this by definition rule out the active sharing of our good news that holistic salvation is possible through God's intervention in Jesus? What if we add the adjectives *empathic, respectful, humble* and *dialogical* to *intervention?* Is that not a kind of "presence"? And suppose we add the words *compassionate, respectful* and *dialogical* to the word *proclamation?* Surely that does not create an oxymoron.

Over the past century, and especially since World War II, there has been a search for a more adequate comprehensive conceptual framework, now called "paradigm," for the church's mission. And as we are entering a new century the quest is being intensified.

The twentieth century began with an evangelism paradigm that assumed that the church was not present. The evangelistic method was confrontive and called for a decision. The message called individuals out of their environing culture into new associations patterned on the missionary's home culture. Such groupings were referred to as "compounds" and effectively separated the converts from their indigenous communities. So the churches in the first instance were associated with Western culture in the minds of local people.

As national self-consciousness reasserted itself in a post-colonial situation, evangelism was increasingly associated with cultural and psychological coercion. And as the third- and fourth-generation churches began to become reaccultur-ated, missiologists articulated a concept of mission as presence. They placed emphasis on personal influence rather than rational and emotional persuasion. Instead of "proclamation," the preferred method of communication was to be "dialogue." "Servanthood," which recognized the validity of the local church as a vital partner, emerged as the ideal posture for mission.

Many important theological assumptions and issues are implicit in this transition. Certainly the emphasis, if not the basic content, of the missionary message was involved. The evangelistic message put emphasis on human sinfulness and God's gracious atonement and forgiveness of our guilt. The presence message stressed that Jesus is God's good news of the world's salvation and invited people to participate.

Theological issues implicit in this transition include the nature of salvation and the importance of a verbalized "gospel"; the nature of the church and the validity of its varied worldwide expressions; the relation of Christianity to other religions; the nature of the human culture and its relation to the kingdom of God. Debates about other, more practical issues like the communicative relation between act and word and the relative value of action and word, or the legitimacy of imposing religious values on another culture, stemmed from basic differences on such issues.

Out of this ongoing discussion a new conceptual framework is emerging, namely, the paradigm of *transformation*, which I want to describe further in the following chapters.[1] My thesis is that the church's mission is agapaic intervention following the pattern of God's intervention in Christ. Its organizations for voluntary social service and evangelistic missions share a common mandate: to take nonviolent initiative in a troubled, alienated world to reconcile and transform its violent, unjust and abusive patterns—in short, to introduce the kingdom of God as a real human possibility. In this paradigm "inculturalization" of the gospel becomes a strategic goal of mission.

The church does not send its missioners into the various parts of the world merely to be respectfully and sympathetically present, to give material and economic humanitarian aid, or merely to "save souls from the burning," as an earlier slogan put it. And it must be added, their goal is not to "plant churches" after the manner of the old missionary compounds. At their best, all these activities must be seen as only tactical strategies to achieve the goal.

The goal of the church is the transformation of human individuals and cultures according to the patterns set forth in Jesus' announcement of the kingdom of God. The church is composed of all who already recognize and acknowledge the dominion of God's rule as it was announced by Jesus. Its missioners are to be *catalytic* and *dialogical* change agents. This is fundamentally implicit in their Christian identity as a part of the "God Movement" in history: the kingdom of God inaugurated by Jesus Christ.

Catalytic Change Agents

In the field of development we are well past the notion that pristine primitive cultures should not be changed. Change is necessary and inevitable in every human culture, and in fact it has taken place from time immemorial. But one senses a certain loss of nerve in some Western Christian voluntary-service programs. Reacting to older imperialistic patterns and sensitive to local cultures, as, indeed, they should be, personnel are reluctant to identify themselves as change agents.

To be effective change agents they must be persuaded that Christian organizations have a unique vision, a viable perspective and effective strategy. They must share a vision for *koinonia*—the New Testament vision of a community based on a self-giving politics of love *(agape).*[2] Further, they need a conceptual foundation and rationale, and for religious organizations that means an adequate theological basis. And they must be confident that the *koinonia* vision truly fits the human situation, so that they need not simply copy secular economic and political patterns in order to succeed.

The two questions that Christian development organizations should ask are what kinds of changes such a *koinonia* vision necessitates and how such changes can be induced. These two questions are, of course, closely related. In the following chapters we will examine them in more detail. But first I want to explain some basic assumptions and conceptions that underlie my thesis.

Recently the metaphor of a catalytic agent has gained some attention by advocates of "people-centered development" like David Korten.[3] Within certain limitations it is a useful metaphor for specifically Christian voluntary organizations. First, then, let me explain what I mean by *catalytic.* In chemistry, of which I know very little, a catalytic agent is a substance that induces change without compounding with and changing the molecular structure of its host elements. Catalysis, then, is a process of modification, of releasing the host element from inhibitive obstructions and inducing intrinsic changes in it.

There are several limitations to the metaphor if taken too literally. In most chemical situations the catalytic agent is not affected by the reaction in the host elements, whereas in participatory development we certainly expect the agents to be changed along with the people with whom they work.

Also in some reactions the effect of the catalyst is unpredictable, and if the catalyst is inappropriate the reaction ceases when the agent is withdrawn. Such contingencies might provide a kind of allegory for the dangers of inducing social change, but there are some catalytic agents that do condition the outcome and set in motion a change reaction that continues in the original elements. In using the metaphor I am underscoring the nonobtrusive, enabling character of authentic Christian action for social change.[4]

I would describe a social catalyst, then, as a change agent that induces desired modifications which are integral and intrinsic to the well-being of the host culture. The implication is that although the changes are desirable and desired, there are inhibiting elements that have prevented the changes from taking place. The catalyst attempts to work respectfully and unintrusively to reduce inhibiting elements and induce changes that will enhance the host culture.

Dialogical Partnership

My second term, *dialogical*, adds a supporting metaphor from communication. Dialogue is the method of social catalysis. It is first of all a relationship before it is an activity—a relationship in which one is open to and respectful of the partner. It seeks to avoid all imposition. David Lochhead points out that it is a relationship implicit in the Christian concept of *agape*.[5] The evangelical goal of dialogue is respectful yet frank and sincere communication aimed at establishing voluntary human community on its highest possible moral and spiritual level. It is the means by which the inner rationale (the logos) of the Christian position is most effectively communicated (1 Pet 3:15).

In order to have a genuine dialogue, several things are necessary. First, the dialogical partners must have clear self-identities. It is extremely difficult to dialogue with a "nobody."

Second, they must be willing to sincerely identify with and listen to each other. Such identification does not mean uncritical agreement. Rather, it means an empathic willingness to put oneself in others' place and see from their perspective.

Third, dialogical partners must be willing to share frankly and intelligently from their own experience. Remember, the goal of catalytic dialogue is not to find the lowest common denominator but to generate change toward the highest common denominator. Although I have not been using theological terminology, this is the heart of what could be called "incarnational disclosure." Jesus' approach to incipient followers was inherently dialogical. He spent thirty years learning their language and two years in dialogue with them.

Presence as Parousia

This brings us to the concept of "presence." What do we mean by *presence* as a missiological term? Much of the debate about presence as a service or mission strategy stems from the word's ambiguity. So we should begin by noting that in its missiological use the word has a strong theological association.

The New Testament word is *parousia,* which is translated coming, arrival or presence. In theology we speak of Christ's first and second parousia. Thus the concept of presence is closely associated with Christ's incarnation in the first instance and with the final realization of God's purposes at the end of history. The Christ has come (Jesus), is coming (Holy Spirit) and will come (messianic consummation). The parousia is active presence moving history toward God's goal.

Thus in New Testament terms, presence indicates a participatory identification with others, but identification within an eschatological context. (*Eschatology* indicates a historical movement toward God's goal for humankind.) By definition, then, the goal of missionary presence is movement toward God's purpose for humanity. It suggests a kind of catalytic intervention with an intended outcome beyond the status quo.[6] What we must remember is that we are only secondary change agents in this process. God's Spirit is the primary change agent (Jn 15:26), and we too need to be changed even as we are being used by the Spirit.[7]

Such a theological understanding of presence leaves us with many practical questions. What does it mean to be truly present to someone? What is involved in being a crosscultural presence? When we speak of the significance of "presence," whose or what presence do we mean? And how is that presence to be identified?

Much of the debate about the effectiveness of presence treats it simply as a mode or strategy of service. It speaks to the question of how I as an individual should present myself in the mission context. For example, shall I be present as an exemplary humanitarian servant? an expert with helpful technical knowledge to share? an instructor? an evangelist? a compassionate Christian ready to share burdens?[8]

Actually, it is virtually impossible to be present only as a private person. Simply entering into a situation from the outside raises questions of where we have come from and whom we represent. Further, a Western origin almost inevitably raises a presumption of suspicion. We inevitably carry a sociocultural identity that affects the presence we project. For example, we learned in India that house servants have a favorable bias toward Americans in contrast to British. As Americans we experienced that favor before anyone actually learned to know us as persons.

Our presence may be perceived as a representative of an institutional North American church program, such as World Vision International, Mennonite Central Committee or Church World Service. It may be a vaguer identity of Western liberal Christianity which is perceived essentially as a sympathetic neutral presence. Or perchance it is a more personable, newly established presence of a local fellowship of confessing Christians.

The organizational identity that we represent will almost certainly project the presence of a "mission" or "project." How does that affect the possibility of real identification? One Japanese church leader raised the question "What is the difference between the missionaries and the Japanese church leaders?" And he answered his own rhetorical question, "After a while the missionaries go home." In any case, we must be careful not to confuse our organizational presence with the Presence we have come to re-present. We do not want to leave the impression that the presence of the Spirit of Christ leaves when we go.

The manner of our presence is also part of our identity. For example, tourists have a definite presence and identity. What kind of presence is indicated in our role, attitude and pattern of relationships? Is it a managerial presence? a presence of power and privilege? a serving presence? a sympathizing presence? an official presence? a patronizing presence? a learner's presence? a teaching presence? On several occasions when I was first introduced into a new situation and culture I was asked, "Well, what did you come to teach us?" Of course I was a teacher by profession, but the servant-teacher does not presume to define the teaching situation. The missioners, both missionaries and service workers, who preceded me had left the impression that missionaries are "teachers" with an agenda.

However we perceive ourselves, it is difficult to avoid stereotypes. We may be perceived as religious proselytizers. In Japan *senkyoshi,* the word for missionary, certainly had this last connotation. Project workers are far more likely to be identified as developers whose goal is economic growth and modernization than as priests come to share the cross of people in poverty. As a Christian presence, missioners must be both self-aware and culturally sensitive.

Most Christians claim in some sense to be a priestly presence mediating the salvific presence of Christ. If that is our aim, how do we accomplish it? Some years ago I visited a Roman Catholic project among the Muslims of Garisa, Kenya. A monastic order was running a secondary-education program for Muslim children, and on the basis of theological as well as pragmatic principles they carefully avoided influencing children to become Christians. In fact, they strongly discouraged conversion. They justified their presence simply as a worshiping, sacramental presence. "The sacramental presence of Christ in the Eucharist sanctifies the work and brings salvation into the situation," they told me.

In contrast to this approach most evangelical, or fundamentalist, Christians would insist on the importance of "proclamation" or evangelism in such a situation. They emphasize the necessity of an explicitly theological presence that requires a verbal witness. Christ as the crucified and risen Savior who died for the sins of the world must be presented and received in order for salvation to be effective. The Spirit of peace and love must be explicitly related to the historical atonement made by Jesus before the Spirit is free to do God's healing/saving work. Simply serving in the Spirit of Jesus as his sacramental representatives is considered an ambiguous witness.

In an attempt to balance the priestly and evangelistic parameters of mission, early Anabaptists emphasized the witness of the Spirit of Christ manifested in the lifestyle as well as proclamation of his followers. Following the example of Paul (Phil 3:8-11), they emphasized the unity of knowing and doing. Knowing Christ requires participation in his "sufferings," that is, the lifestyle that led to the cross. In the words of Menno Simons, Christians must "bear the heavy cross of Christ" as an essential element of their witness to Christ. There must be no "triumphalism," no coercive manipulation. Where there is no "cross," the witness is distorted. As Kosuke Koyama in his book by the same title reminds us, there is "no handle on the cross."

This is the theological assumption behind service "in the name of Christ." To act in the name of Christ first means to act as a servant in the style and under the authority of Christ. We do this in faith that the promised Spirit of Christ, the Paraclete, will make God present in the actions and words of his representatives. To serve in the name of Christ means to serve explicitly as his representatives, signifying his presence and power at work inaugurating the rule of God. And this leads to a second dimension of meaning, namely, that the power at work is the power of Jesus, not our own. The first apostles were quite adamant about this!

But this raises a very real question. How do we communicate that it is God's presence and power that is the basic reality and not merely our own personal religious presence or that of some service organization? As I have said, such a presence is the work of the Spirit; but from the human side, what demeanor, attitude, action, word, program or relationship will communicate the Spirit's presence? Can we do it with attitudes and actions only? Can we communicate the presence of Christ without sharing the story of Jesus? What is the role of proclamation? Is there a time to speak and a time not to speak? Can we separate actions and words? Is not speaking an act?

Some years ago in Chengdu, China, my wife and I were buying wall hangings from a local artist who knew a little English. While we were trying to rivet his Chinese name into our minds, he said simply, "My Christian name is Timothy." It was as if he had quietly drawn the fish symbol in the sand! His unassuming verbal identification changed the whole relationship paradigm. It gave his pictures of birds and flowers a new ambience.

With these questions in mind we turn to a more detailed consideration of the spiritual character of all Christian ministries, the spiritual formation necessary for effective salvific intervention, the nature of the evangelization process as we attempt to inculturate the gospel, and the nature of the world system that we are confronting in our ministries.

3

Reorienting
the Conceptual
Framework for
Mission

•••

*T*HERE IS A GROWING CONSENSUS THAT WE SHOULD MOVE
from a concept of development as simply economic or
industrial growth to development as social transformation.
Already in the mid-1970s, Edgar Stoez wrote that development must not be understood as urbanization, industriali-
zation, modernization or Westernization. "People are what
development is all about. . . . Development is the conscien-
tization process by which people are awakened to opportunities within their reach." He insisted that it must be an
integrated community process and that attitudes must be
changed.[1] This was a positive protest against what was in fact
happening in too many politically sponsored programs.

In his *Getting to the Twenty-first Century* David Korten
writes, "The elimination of unjust structures depends on the
emergence of an alternative human consciousness." Having
urged that "the need to define an alternative vision of

development" for voluntary action by individuals and organizations is fundamental, he concludes, "This is perhaps the most central of religious missions, and a far worthier challenge for religiously oriented voluntary development organizations than the distribution of charity to victims of the failure of spiritual teaching."[2]

Korten is quite specific about the nature of the necessary reorientation. It requires a redefinition of "living well." The good life must be understood as a social, intellectual and spiritual quality of life rather than a higher standard of material consumption. Accordingly, motivational patterns must be changed. No longer can we assume that as the economy grows the rich have a right to get proportionally richer. Development can no longer succeed by appealing to the essential egoism and greed of both individual and organized humankind. Understandably, Korten is not overly optimistic about achieving such a radical reorientation.

The obvious failure of international economic development strategies to close the gap between rich and poor nations, along with the growing ecological crisis that has resulted from the attempt, raises questions about underlying presuppositions. Development's failure discredits the liberal assumption of the essential goodness of human beings and the adequacy of rational self-interest as a control mechanism. It challenges the assumption that a free, self-regulating economic system will serve the interests of the poor, or that the powerful will protect the weak. Such a challenge indicates the need for a much more radical approach to the "development" of human society. Indeed, it calls for a transformation of the human psyche and society—an alternative consciousness for both individuals and the social order.

If this analysis is correct—and I find it very difficult to refute—then it implies the need for a radical change in the goals and strategy of most Christian voluntary-service organizations. While mainline church and parachurch development organizations acknowledge the importance of religious and ethical motivation, they have patterned their strategies and goals after secular models. Their underlying theological assumptions have been essentially those of Enlightenment humanism and theistic evolution. In a very perceptive article David Wright points out that churches have too readily taken their cues from national political and economic strategies and goals.[3]

Such an analysis may seem to indicate that evangelicals have been right all along by insisting on the necessity of a spiritual rebirth. Indeed, they are correct in their insistence on a spiritual conversion, but they have not understood conversion as an alternative consciousness that effects a social as well as individual transformation. Although the theological climate is changing, evangelicals still often understand spiritual conversion as strictly an individual, theocentric change that affects one's personal ethics.[4] Social justice is not anticipated as an end of religious conversion. The slogan "Changed lives change the world" has been used to justify a lack of social emphasis, not as a promise of social justice, even if only incrementally. In such a view social justice can result only from Christ's cataclysmic arrival and violent confrontation of evil at the end of the age.

The evangelical paradigm continues to work with the traditional dualism of spiritual and material-social. For this reason evangelicals have been very slow to legitimate "social action" programs that work for an "evangelical" transformation of social and economic systems. Even evangelical organizations that have tried to stay under the umbrella of the church have been granted, grudgingly at best, a "parachurch" standing.[5] Speaking theologically, what is needed is a new, holistic view of the psychophysical human person as a spiritual being.

Conceptual Frameworks for a Transformational Paradigm

The concern of experts outside the church for a reorientation of development programs underscores the need for a more genuinely holistic conceptual framework for the church's mission. It presses us to move beyond both the dualism of traditional orthodoxy and Enlightenment rationalism *and* the reductionism of secular positivism. We need a concept of the spiritual as constituent of and integral to understanding human beings in their society.

The first chapter referred to three paradigms that have controlled mission thinking over the past century. The first of these, the evangelism paradigm, is clearly based on a dualistic view of human beings. The presence paradigm implies a modified dualism that recognizes the intricate interrelation between the spiritual and the sociophysical. A transformation paradigm requires a further unified view of humans as spiritual beings in the image of God. A brief review of the progression of these conceptual frameworks as they have affected the church's voluntary aid and service programs will help us to uncover the locus of our concern.

In the post-Civil War years, the traditional concept of missions based on a postmillennial view of eschatology was challenged by a renewed premillennialism. Postmillennialism held that Jesus would return to reign on the earth after ("post") the church, in the power of the Spirit, had established the kingdom of God. The task of missions was to extend Christendom and thus prepare the way of the Lord.

The new premillennialism was extremely literalistic and oriented to the "end time." It made a sharp dispensational distinction between the church and the kingdom of God. The church was understood to be a purely spiritual presence of the kingdom. The kingdom as a social reality was to be established by the return of Jesus Christ to rule with a "rod of iron." In its most extreme form it virtually restricted the mission of the church to the spiritual renewal of individuals through the preaching of the atonement of Christ. This was the new definition of evangelism, in contrast to the earlier concept of evangelization by establishing the church and winning converts to it.

Evangelism was conceived as persuasion by emotional and rational means like those employed in the revivalist movement that set about to win the American frontier for Christ. Needless to say, not all churches accepted this definition of evangelism as the conceptual framework for missions, but it was extremely influential and pervasive in conservative Protestant circles.

Some, becoming increasingly sensitive to what they considered the cultural and psychological coercion of this approach, emphasized the simple "proclamation" of the gospel story and rationalized social and educative services as a kind of "preevangelism." They put great effort into translating the Scriptures, so that the message of the Bible itself in local languages would be the primary influence. And in a final stage of self-understanding, some leaders like John R. W. Stott insisted that social service as an act of *agape* (Christlike love) must also be accepted as proclamation of the gospel.

Slowly a new paradigm of "presence" emerged (see chapter one). As I have noted, this understanding of mission emphasizes agapaic identification with others and demonstration of the new kingdom reality as the authentication of the message. While proclamation is not discarded, new stress is given to dialogue as a means of communicating the gospel. And new importance is given to faith in Christ as an experience of sociospiritual relationship. In this paradigm "servanthood" provides the motivation and rationale for mission, and social services take on new significance as witness to the gospel.

Certainly this accent on presence is important as a corrective to the more imperious pressure for conversion which too often included a Western cultural component extraneous to the gospel. However, it misses something of the dynamic of the gospel as a change agent in human culture. The apostle Paul experienced and preached the gospel as a transforming, enabling disclosure of the power of God in human life. He expected it to change human relationships and create a just and loving community. Transformation as a new conceptual foundation for mission can provide this good news perspective to our proclamation, presence and service.

When we envision our goal as transformation of human society after the pattern of love and justice demonstrated in Jesus, several things immediately become obvious. First, the goal requires a radically altered consciousness on the part of both the haves and the have-nots, the donors and the recipients. Second, given the limitations and conflicting wants of individuals, we cannot directly design and fabricate such a goal. A humanly invented motivation for what Korten calls a "just," "sustainable," and "inclusive" socioeconomic order has thus far eluded us! While the goal includes technical, social and psychological changes that we may promote, it requires a basic spiritual intervention and conversion over which we have little or no control.

Such spiritual transformation is an inclusive state that encompasses both deed and motivation. It is not merely an altered motivation or intention in the causal sequence between knowing and doing. On the other hand, it is not merely a cultural or technological change. It is what Paul described as a social-spiritual transformation (Gal 3:26-28) and called "a new creation" (Gal 6:15). He also spoke of it as "faith working through love" (Gal 5:6).[6]

In a transformation paradigm, our human intervention is indirect and vicarious. It is indirect in the sense that we cannot go with preconstructed solutions to be imposed on the situation.[7] It is vicarious in the sense that we must become one with those whom we would serve. Christlike servants must take upon themselves the basic cultural identity of those whom they would serve. In this Jesus is the model. His two-year ministry ending in death and resurrection was necessarily preceded by thirty years of vicarious bonding with his people. That is why the earliest Christian theologians emphasized the incarnation as the means of our salvation and not simply Jesus' death as a divine substitutionary intervention. The New Testament word that describes this kind of vicarious intervention is *agape.*

All this suggests that the communicative strategy for a transformative ministry must be *koinonaic* and *demonstrative. Koinonia* has both the meaning of sharing *with* and sharing *in,* or participation. In koinonaic ministry we share what we ourselves have found to be transforming, and we participate in the new reality of the reconciled community. Demonstration of the new social reality is absolutely integral to such a ministry. Jesus communicated the inner meaning of salvation by healing the sick, feeding the hungry, casting out demonic forces, freeing those bound by tradition and instructing his followers in the new freedom and possibility of the kingdom of God. Only at the end of his ministry did he disclose his messianic secret—the secret that we use as a kind of saving mantra.

If it is objected that the postresurrection message is one

of messianic proclamation, it should be noted that the Day
of Pentecost represents the climax of Jesus' life. He was
proclaimed Messiah on the grounds of a shared knowledge
of his life—a life of "doing good and healing all who were
oppressed by the devil" (Acts 10:38). Further, the apostles
continued such a healing ministry as a fundamental witness
to his messianic claim. The messianic proclamation *follows*
a demonstration of Jesus' saving efficacy. I am not arguing
against a clear witness to Jesus as the Christ, but for sensitivity and authenticity in the witness process.

Change and Change Agents: An Incarnational Style

The very concept of "gospel," or good news *(euangelion),*
implies intervention. As Bishop D. T. Niles said many years
ago, "Evangelism is one beggar telling another beggar where
to find bread." But in a religiously pluralistic world we have
lost some of the moral imperative of this implicit mandate.
In our postmodern setting we can feel the obligation to share
the advantages of modern medicine more keenly than the
obligation to share the good news of alternative community.
We find it much easier to share emergency material aid than
to address the cultural-spiritual problems that have caused
that emergency.

  This sensitivity in itself is not necessarily bad. While we
recognize that the good news "to the poor" (Lk 4:18) is to
be shared, we have become increasingly sensitive to the way
we enter situations of need. Clearly we must learn to be
much more sensitive in our intervention. A "gospel" intervention is not intrusive! It must not be domineering or
authoritarian. Like most medical doctors, who prefer nonintrusive intervention when at all possible, we must be "wise
as serpents and innocent as doves" (Mt 10:16; cf. Lk 10:3).

  For at least the last quarter-century we have used the term

incarnational to describe our missionary and service stance. That, of course, is a good word and clearly implies that we must follow the pattern of Christ himself. But it may imply a presumption of human ability. We must never forget that Christ's incarnation required a miracle! Thus I am suggesting *catalytic* as a less presumptuous synonym of *incarnational* in order to indicate the way in which we attempt to bring about change.

The fact of cultural change itself is not problematic. As I have noted, cultures are dynamic, highly adaptive and constantly adjusting to new circumstances. Sometimes the change agent is from within the culture (innovation), sometimes from outside (diffusion). What kind of change and how that change is brought about is our concern. Indeed, change (*metanoia* or repentance) is at the heart of the gospel. But from a Christian perspective the nature, goals and process of that change are integrally intertwined. As the philosopher John Dewey observed, the means contain and condition the ends.

Our concern is to be *nonintrusive*. Intrusion indicates an uninvited forcible entry. To intrude is "to thrust oneself in without invitation, permission or welcome" *(Webster's Ninth New Collegiate Dictionary)*. For example, although the United Nations' intervention in Somalia was for a good cause, it was intrusive. We must carefully consider what kind of "entering" is wrongful and offensive from the gospel perspective. Like our Master, we go not to judge but to save (Jn 12:47).

According to an incarnational model where the change agent comes from the outside, it is especially important that innovations should not be forced or manipulated. As Louis Luzbetak says of applied anthropology, "We wish through cooperation, rather than manipulation of any kind, to influence the society's patterns of behavior." Innovations should be culturally relevant and authentic. "Whenever possible [they should] be presented as something that will complete and perfect the existing cultural design."[8]

Thus the would-be change agent must be ready to adapt to the host culture, especially in its "overt" aspects, the physical and psychological-social. "Covert" or ideational aspects, such as beliefs, thought patterns and emotional evaluations, require empathy and honesty. One should view the cultural expressions "emically," that is, from the inside, rather than bring foreign cultural norms and meanings into the context as an immediate basis of judgment.

This calls for respect, understanding, honest self-examination and nonthreatening authentic communication. It does not require an indiscriminate adoption of the host culture ("going native") in the hope of being accepted. Indeed, such a response is likely to be superficial and may even be dishonest.

Such a stance does not necessarily imply that there are no absolutes and every cultural expression is as valid as every other. Rather, it implies that all human cultures, including the Christian cultures of the West, are at best relative expressions of God's absolute norm of *agape*, namely, self-giving mutuality and interdependence. Their ideational patterns or worldviews, their moral traditions, their sociopolitical organization, their economic systems—all are imperfect.

To say that all cultural systems are relative implies that they *all*, including Christian culture, have dysfunctional elements that degrade and alienate human beings. It simply is not true that every cultural pattern or religious value is equally functional and effective for authentic human development. The Gospel of John refers to such elements as "darkness," and when "light" comes, darkness is judged and, hopefully, dispersed (Jn 1:5). Changes are needed in every culture in order for humanity to reach its full potential under God.

If we use this metaphor of light, we must remember that it is not *our* light shining in *their* darkness. We do not go with our flashlights to search out the dark crevices of their culture. The deficiencies, inequities, injustice and violence of our own Western "Christian" culture throw considerable doubt on our right to intervene at all. And if we intervene in a judgmental posture, surely the words of Paul to his first-century Jewish compatriots will apply to us: "You, then, that teach others, will you not teach yourself?" (Rom 2:21). We must be careful to heed the warning of Jesus not to try to take the speck of dust out of the other culture's eye while ignoring the log in our own culture's eye (Mt 7:3).

Like the proverbial cock crowing at sunrise, we merely herald the dawning light that warms and exposes all human culture. Intercultural experience itself can open our eyes to the "dawn from on high" upon our own darkness, giving "light to those who sit in darkness and in the shadow of death, to guide our feet in the way of peace" (Lk 1:78-79). Standing outside our culture should enable us to better evaluate it.

But even more important is the realization that every culture, imperfect as it may be, is a human creation and has the potential of expressing authentic human community under the covenant of the Creator. We do not approach cultures other than our own as though they were demonic. One is reminded of the retort of some nineteenth-century missionaries when they were urged to study Hindu culture more thoroughly. "This culture," they replied, "is of the devil. We did not come to study it, but to destroy it." But demons do not create culture: humans do. The good news of the incarnation is that every human culture has the potential to host God!

As change agents, we are attempting to introduce innovations that will change dysfunctional aspects of the cultural system, whether they be economic, social or religious and moral values and practices. We are not simply trying to help individuals escape the system. Of course we begin with individuals, but our aim is to introduce innovations into the system through changed individuals and relationships. That is why the contextualization, or as the Roman Catholics put it, the inculturation, of the new personal-social possibility (gospel) is so necessary. This is the reason for our insistence on the change agent's identification with or incarnation into the culture.

4

What Kind of Intervention?

Defining the "Spiritual"

••

*I*N THIS CHAPTER WE WILL EXPLORE THE ESSENTIALLY spiritual nature of the human family and what this implies about the kind of intervention and change we hope to effect. In our zeal to remedy the ills of the world, like Martha of old, we may have become encumbered with "much serving."

Among the various religious services and aid organizations there are differences of opinion about the theological nature of the mission. The immediate need, whether it be abused children, starvation or degrading poverty, has been so pressing that we have not spent much time thinking through a theological rationale. Our missiology has been largely implicit and arrived at pragmatically.

Some development strategies emphasize economic and industrial development; others insist on a broader social approach. Some Christian agencies still insist that service must be in the context of an explicit evangelistic proclamation, that it can be justified only as a form of evangelism. Others would see it as "preevangelism." Others would justify compassionate aid given in response to God's love as a Christian end in itself. And still others emphasize the broadly religious and humanitarian character of social service and development.

We must constantly underscore and strengthen the Christian spiritual nature of our mission and goals, in contrast to their more pragmatic and programmatic character. The debates whether the goals of development should be primarily economic or social and whether evangelism should take precedence over service need to be grounded in an understanding of human nature. Indeed, each approach embraces and proceeds upon an implicit anthropology, whether admitted or not.

A missiology adequate to carry us into the future must be one that encompasses both mission boards and service organizations. Both kinds of organizations struggle with the spiritual-physical schizophrenia of our sharply dualistic cultural heritage. In reaction against a type of spirituality and evangelism that seem reductionist and narrow, we struggle to find an authentic, holistic alternative.[1] We speak of "holistic ministries," but we find it hard to integrate the spiritual, psychological and physical dimensions. We realize that we begin to lose our integrity when we insist on two separate parallel tracks, one for service and one for evangelism. But we hesitate to describe the aspects of ministry as tributaries flowing together to make one great river. Such a unified missiology would have important implications for mission boards as well as service organizations.

The lack of integration is evident in our approach to economic development. Christian agencies have largely assumed that a "free market" economy is the basic paradigm for *Christian* relief and development work. This model is based on Adam Smith's theory of work and economic consumption, and the concept of humans as "economic animals" which it implies. It assumes that individual initiative and competition are the necessary motivating factors and that rational self-interest will control the process. Thus it promotes "privatization" and the right to "private profit," even at the immediate expense of the group. It is confident that in the long run rational mutuality will prevail.

But are human beings rational "economic animals" who will put communal justice ahead of private profit? Certainly individual initiative is to be encouraged, and granting the right to private property and enterprise clearly does that. But how do we ensure an equitable distribution and a spirit of mutual sharing? What the agencies seem to have forgotten is that even Adam Smith's "invisible hand" of self-interest was presumed to justly regulate the economic process only when it began with a fair distribution of economic assets. It was not intended as a means of *creating* a just economic balance.[2]

Christian aid organizations have downsized, contextualized and personalized this economic development model. They have made the poor the direct object of their concern. They have worked self-consciously in the context of local churches of host countries to improve the lives of those they attempt to help. They have added explicit religious ministries, such as supplying Christian literature, making loans for local church projects or providing teachers for Bible schools and seminaries. All of these things reflect a spiritual concern, but the organizations have still relied on self-interest as the basic operating motive.

These attempts of church agencies to modify the "free market" paradigm are commendable. But the failure to narrow the gap between the rich and poor, the increase of civil strife, new understandings about the dynamics of culture, new insights from liberation theology and new practical experiences in contexts of violence challenge us to reexamine our assumptions about human nature. We must explore more critically what kind of "development" will be effective and what are the motivational springs for social transformation. This requires that we be more explicit about the fundamentally spiritual nature of our purpose and program strategies.

What Kind of Intervention?

To determine what kind of intervention is needed, we must first analyze and make a diagnosis of the human situation. How do we perceive those we serve, and how do we assess the problem we wish to solve? Is the problem basically maldistribution of the world's goods? Then finding ways to share material aid and working out fair trade policies constitute the solution. Is it technological? Then appropriate technology and "development" would seem to be the answer. Is it competition, conflict and violence? Then mediation. Is it spiritual poverty and deviancy? Then the healing of the individual and social psyche, which the New Testament refers to as *metanoia* (a change of heart) or conversion (a radical renewal and reorientation of life), will be required. Of course the actual situational problems are complex and may vary significantly. But we bring basic presuppositions and definitions that condition our approach to each situation.

Reflecting on this question, David Korten writes, "The human spirit must be strengthened to the point that greed and egotism play a less dominant role." He observes, as I noted in the last chapter, that this is perhaps the most central mission of religiously oriented voluntary development organizations. Then he adds:

This leads to a sobering realization. The elimination of unjust structures depends on the emergence of an alternative human consciousness. This consciousness must view power not as a club to be used in the service of personal aggrandizement, but rather as a gift to be held in stewardship to the service of the community and the human and spiritual fulfillment of all people—especially the powerless.[3]

The biblical-Christian view is that human beings are spiritual covenant creatures. Aristotle, who was a Greek contemporary of the Hebrew prophets, held that they are social animals distinguished by rationality. For him social cooperation is based on rational friendship *(philia)* or mutual self-interest. But the prophets insisted that humans are creatures bound together by covenant responsibility that transcends individual self-interest, however rational. The ultimate bond is *ḥesed* or *agapē*, self-giving love that is willing to go beyond the stipulations of strict mutuality.

In modern psychological parlance, we refer to human beings as "psychosomatic" units. But the human individual is more than a single unified body of mental and physical processes and activities. If we use this kind of terminology we need to describe human beings as *pneumosomatic,* that is, creatures whose mental-physical bodies *(sōma)* have a transcendent or spiritual *(pneumatikos)* destiny in God. Our ultimate self-identity is found in our relationship to God, not only to our physical world and one another.

The task of redefining the spiritual nature of the mission that this implies is complicated by the controversy between mainline and evangelical movements. On the one hand, religious pluralism challenges the idea that there is a normative pattern of human spirituality. And its assumption that salvation is attainable through all religions challenges an explicitly christocentric base for Christian intervention. Does Christianity have a distinct spirituality and ethic that should guide us and be reflected in our program priorities and strategies? How can the unique contribution of Christ be introduced into the various cultures with their own valid (for them) spiritualities? What does it mean for local organizations and programs to say that what we do is "in the name of Christ"? How necessary is it that the name of Jesus be verbally identified and attached to compassionate service?

On the other hand, evangelicals have rejected pluralism and have insisted on the exclusive authority of Christ *as he is understood in the Western evangelical tradition.* They hold that Christian intervention must be explicitly christocentric. Only Christian spirituality can relate us to the "true God" of the Bible. Thus verbal proclamation of the gospel and the formation of churches as we know them in the West are the priority. Indeed, there is great hesitancy to identify and cooperate even with other traditional Christian groups. An authentic Christian spirituality necessarily requires a "church-planting" approach in which the spiritual and social are clearly distinguished and priority is given to the spiritual.[4]

This raises a different set of questions. How explicit need we be in affirming Jesus Christ as the only valid Savior? How do we identify authentic Christian spirituality? On what basis do we identify and cooperate with Christian churches of other cultures in our local work? How are the social, cultural and physical aspects of life included in the Christian understanding of the salvation proclaimed in Christ? How are the healing, reconciling, economic sharing, peacemaking and social justice aspects of life related to "spiritual" salvation? And is there a specific priority and order to these dimensions? Must we follow a strategic order in witnessing to the kingdom?

I have stated my own perspective in the second chapter: that the church's voluntary service organizations, including both missions and aid, are institutions for agapaic intervention in situations of need. When I use the word *agape,* I am referring to a specifically Christian concept that was embodied in the life and ministry of Jesus Christ. When I say that we are "interventionist," I am simply identifying the church's mission as the continuing mission of God begun in Christ's incarnational ministry. Jesus Christ is God's intervention into the human scene, and the church through the presence and empowerment of the Spirit of Christ continues that intervention ministry.[5]

Defining the Spiritual

Before further talk about a spiritual God-dimension can be very useful in our service strategy, we will need to define what we mean by the spiritual dimension.

The human spirit is not a separate part of our individual being the way an arm is part of the body. It is not something distinct from and added to our bodies and minds and somehow more essential than they are. Rather, *spirit* is a holistic term. *Spirit* refers to the whole human being in his or her wholeness made "in the image of God." We cannot be described ultimately as "economic animals" or "tool-making animals," but as "spiritual animals." The whole self is more than the sum of its parts. In theological terms, it is a creation of the Spirit of God and shares in that Spirit. As Paul puts it in Romans 8:16, God's Spirit in communication with our spirit assures us that we are God's children, that is, "in God's image."

Speaking of the spiritual as an observable dimension of our experience, we can identify the following "intimations of our spiritual being"—with apologies to William Wordsworth:

1. The *self-understanding* of both ourselves and others as children of God in the image of the Creator. This is the characteristic that, for example, made it worth the late Mother Teresa's self-sacrifice to give a fellow human being a meaningful death in a compassionate setting.

2. The *personal quality* of human beings that opens them to the transcendent dimensions and moral demands of life: submission to and trust in God (faith), which enables them to put compassion and self-sacrifice (love) ahead of their own egocentric ("fleshly") desires and fears.

3. The *intuition of a destiny* beyond physical mortality (hope), which leads them to risk death in the pursuit of human value and well-being.

4. The *self-awareness* that humankind's highest identity and ultimate meaning are found in solidarity *(koinonia)* under the loving dominion of the God whom Jesus called Father.

So the spiritual encompasses the texture of our total being. It is the distinctly human dimension of both our individual and our social being. We might speak of it as both a transcendent and a depth dimension that involves us in relationship to God and to each other—what the Bible calls the "heart," the personal depth of our being. It expresses itself most clearly in our self-image, which is simply the underside of our God-image, and in the motivations, underlying assumptions and rationalizations that create human cultures.

With this understanding of humanity's essential nature, it becomes obvious that the human problem is fundamentally "spiritual." Or to put it negatively, it is not simply technological, political or economic. But in order to understand what this means, we need a new conceptualization of spirit.

To say that the human problem is fundamentally spiritual does not locate the problem in some religious or mystical realm, but rather locates the material, economic, physiological and psychological dimensions within the context of the larger holistic and transcendent reality. It defines the problem not in reductionist but in holistic terms, not simply as behavioral patterns but in terms of personal-social dynamics and values.

If, then, the human problem is basically a spiritual problem and we do not deal with it, our relief, development and mediation work will be superficial. As Louis Luzbetak observes, "Technical development by no means implies that a technologically advanced society is necessarily able to deal more successfully with its social problems or that it has a greater capacity to cope with its ideational environment more satisfactorily than a less technologically developed society."[6] Or as Walter Wink puts it, "Structural change is not enough; the heart and soul must also be freed, forgiven, energized."[7]

Our goals and strategies must include the elements of culture that inhibit and defeat the goals of holistic human development (which I take to be a nontheological description of salvation). These are "spiritual" inhibitions—fatalism, depression of spirit, self-depreciation (believing oneself a "nobody"), a sense of powerlessness resulting from internalized oppression, structures and values that create codependency, and self-centered anxiety that often justifies or excuses deceitful and manipulative behavior.

Defining the Change We Want
Terry Alliband, who writes from his experience in India,

makes "modernization" the goal of development. "Modernization is a process in which group prejudices and group-thinking disintegrates, or, at least, is greatly reduced by the forces of individualism. *The individual begins to regard his or her personal fortune as being of greater importance than that of one's hereditary group. . . . This shifting of allegiance is the basic transformation involved in the modernization process.*"[8]

This, he says, demands a "comprehensive human development" approach, not merely technological and economic development. The problem, he says, is one of ongoing motivation, and he sees this as the work of community development overcoming the inhibitions of an oppressive tradition. He holds that the only way to modernize Indian culture is to educate and advance the values of individualism.

Dor Bahadur Bista, a Nepali social anthropologist, implies the same thing in his *Fatalism and Development: Nepal's Struggle for Modernization*. In page after page he documents the virtual impossibility of introducing the benefits of modern technology and a free market into a society like Nepal that is ruled by fatalism and the caste system that was introduced from India. There must be a basic change in personal and cultural values in the direction of modernization.[9]

Certainly this is a valid analysis of the problem development workers face, but I have serious reservations about the authors' proposed solution. At the heart of modern individualism is the assumption that rational self-interest will create the new community. India, with its fatalistic doctrine of karma, is plagued by individualism and a lack of social responsibility. Indeed, the Gandhian social experiment foundered on this rock, and I see little hope that the substitution of modern individualism will remedy the situation.

We need a much more radical solution that can create an alternate consciousness and thus an alternative community. In the words of Jesus, unless such a conversion takes place there is no possibility of seeing, much less entering, the kingdom of God.

What kind of changes does such a "comprehensive human development" entail? In theological terms, the mission is to be an anticipatory sign of and witness to God's rule in history. The development goal is to promote alternative communities of mutual concern, communities of shalom-justice that will operate as salt and light within the present world systems. This will mean motivating and energizing individuals as well as producing corrective structural changes in society. In the terms I have been using, this is clearly a "spiritual" enterprise.

Before pursuing the nature of the cultural and personal transformation necessary to human development, we need to pause and recognize the danger of judging unfamiliar cultural idioms too quickly. And, one might add, this applies as readily to the cultures on our geographical doorstep as to those overseas. America has become the home of many cultures!

Unless we are thoroughly familiar with a culture, we stand in danger of disregarding or even denigrating its customs. We do well to remember the example of the apostle Paul, who said of his own ministry, "I have become all things to all people [of all cultures], that I might by all means save some" (1 Cor 9:22; see vv. 19-23). Indeed, it is the great danger of devaluing a people's culture that makes an incarnational approach so essential to mission.

Nevertheless, to be more concrete I propose five basic social-personal changes that are necessary to holistic trans-formation. In classical orthodox theology these changes have been referred to as "conversion," that is, a turning around, and "repentance," or reorientation. The Greek word for repentance is *metanoia,* which means changing one's orientation to life.

Unfortunately, the terms *conversion* and *repentance* have been devalued by their connotative association with a particular Western religious tradition. In their original setting, however, they described what modern development theorists refer to as "alternative consciousness" and "overcoming the inhibitions of oppressive tradition."

First, individuals must be liberated/converted from inherent patterns of violence and self-seeking in their personal lives. Personal and social patterns of violence are mutually reinforcing and must be rooted out. Violence in this case does not mean simply physical brutality. It includes all forms of deceptive and abusive manipulation of others for one's own purposes. Such violence stems from alienation and fear and is endemic to all human cultures, including that of the development worker.

Second, inhibiting, fatalistic traditions that stifle and repress hope must be exorcised. Indeed, such traditions are the cultural counterpart of the ancient *daimonoi* (intermediate deities or spiritual powers), which were thought to rule the different nations. Tradition is the cultural womb in which both social and individual self-identities are formed. Little wonder that Nicodemus stumbled at such an unimaginable "rebirth," or that Dor Bahadur Bistra despairs of modern development in a fatalistic culture.

Third, oppressive hierarchical social structures that create and maintain the slavery of codependency must be dismantled. This is basically a political task, but it requires a new kind of politics. Individuals must learn self-respect and respect for others as children of God. One of the great words of the apostle Paul is *freedom*. "For freedom Christ has set us free. . . . Do not submit again to a yoke of slavery" (Gal 5:1).

The last two kinds of change relate to the impact of modernity on traditional cultures. Dysfunctional ideologies (superstitions) that rationalize avoidable diseases, disasters and accidents need to be replaced with viable, empirical approaches to nature and physical well-being. Modern Western civilization has desacralized nature. Based on the biblical concept of nature's creatureliness, Western science has assumed that nature is comprehensible, and it has applied techniques of observation and experimentation in the place of mystery and magic. An illustration of the enormous positive change this can make is the virtual eradication of the guinea worm from large parts of Africa through simple experimental techniques.

As in so many other cases, the difficulty in bringing about desirable changes in this area has been exacerbated by the imperious assumptions and attitudes of the West. In our zeal to save lives, we have too often imposed Western methods on traditional ideological systems. Fortunately, Western science itself has become less bound by "natural laws" and increasingly respectful of the incredible variety of human experience. For example, medical researchers have become more open to the value of traditional therapeutic experience and to adapting treatments to cultural situations.

Finally, mutually adapted technologies that will effectively improve the human quality of life need to be introduced. Such a mandate certainly is included under the biblical exhortation to do good to all fellow human beings as well as to one's own family (Gal 6:10). Sharing material aid and medical and other technologies is an elemental component of human interdependence and a strategic part of the Christian mission.

I have stated these necessary changes in our contemporary secular vocabulary, but upon a little reflection the ministry of Jesus itself provides the paradigm for such transformation. He challenged Israel's traditional interpretation of the Mosaic Torah, which underlay the social and political life of Israel (Mt 5:21-48). He called Israel to repent from its trust in the Maccabean sword of deliverance and justice. To accomplish this goal he had to exorcise demonic powers and free the people from their bondage to what Walter Wink has called "the Domination System."[10] Jesus healed the sick and demonstrated authentic divine-human relationships (introduced a new politics). He gave the people bread (emergency aid) and taught them (patient education). Because we have sharply distinguished between the religious and the secular in our modern culture, we often fail to see the "secular" meaning and relevance of Jesus' pattern of ministry.

The ministry of Jesus, for which he gave his life both as martyr and as vicarious representative, was a ministry to individuals in their sociospiritual and physical contexts. He did not simply offer them a spiritual escape. He introduced a new "kingdom," an alternative cultural system. It is simply not enough to change *individuals* economically, culturally or spiritually and leave them to function in the old system. On the other hand, it is futile to change social and economic structures if the hearts of individuals have not changed.

Such holistic *metanoia* is a spiritual transformation, and it is possible only through the motivating power of the Spirit of Christ. The Old Testament prophets and the New Testament are full of references to the inclusive scope of "salvation" or transformation.[11] Loving God is a total life activity involving every aspect of living—material, psychic-personal, social, spiritual.

5

A Christian Spirituality for Intervention Ministries

● ●

*T*WO QUOTATIONS FROM VERY DIFFERENT SOURCES HIGHLIGHT the importance of spirituality for the task of social transformation. The first is by Walter Wink in *Naming the Powers:*

Too often our social action has been as devoid of spirituality as our evangelism has been politically innocuous. . . . Too much of the time we have drawn on secular models of social change without drawing as well on our own rich fund of symbolism and imagery, liturgy, and story. Many dismissed the hymns and gospel songs, the eucharists and prayers of a Martin Luther King, Jr., or Cesar Chavez as merely shrewd accommodations to the subcultures with which they worked. Such critics did not perceive that these were essential forms of struggle in themselves, that the enemy is not always self-evident, that engaging a Power on its own terms guarantees that the victor, whichever it is, will perpetuate the same terms. They did not address themselves to the transcendent One who alone could work changes which do not themselves bear the seeds of new evils.[1]

The next is from Lynn Samaan in "Spiritual Formation for Relief and Development Workers":

Charles H. Kraft related a conversation which Jacob Loewen once had with some of the nationals in Panama regarding values the missionaries had taught them. Sadly, without hesitation they responded, "money." When pressed as to whether they had actually been told these were the most important values they replied, "No, but this is what the missionaries' actions clearly taught" and what they themselves now wanted.[2]

These two vignettes reflect two approaches to the definition and practice of spirituality. Martin Luther King's and Cesar Chavez's movements were overtly social and political, but they were grounded in a Christian spirituality explicitly acknowledged in their practice of nonviolence, prayer and sacramental devotion. In the case of the Panama missionaries, spirituality was narrowly associated with the evangelistic aspect of their mission, and in the eyes of the nationals it did not characterize their actual presence and values.

In the last chapter I tried to redefine the concept of "spirit" and "spiritual." There I said that spirituality describes the texture of our total being and expresses itself in our motivations, way of relating to others, values and rationalizations. That understanding will provide the background for our examination of Christian spirituality in this chapter.

For a long time the word *spirituality* has been suspect among us, and even now it has a vast array of connotations. Many people identify it with a certain kind of religious devotion, such as the sacred heart of Mary or moral piety and Bible study. Then there is what we might call the spirituality of the "Four Spiritual Laws," which identifies it with being a "born-again" Christian—a purely theological virtue. The holiness tradition thinks of spirituality as a special sanctification and holy life. New Age spirituality is defined as communion with the world spirit, being in touch with the higher dimensions of one's inner self and so on. So we must first take time to understand what we mean by the term.

Our sharp dichotomy between the spiritual and the sociophysical has made us suspicious that spirituality may disqualify people for practical, everyday work. We have all heard the old quip "He is so heavenly minded that he is no earthly good." For most Protestants *spiritual* was an epithet suggesting an aura of superpiety, somewhat like *saint* for Roman Catholics. But in the past two decades Roman Catholic writers and Protestants like David Bosch and Richard Foster have refurbished the concepts of spiritual formation and spiritual disciplines so that they have become more usable.[3]

Barbara Hendricks and Thomas Clarke, writing of spirituality in the Roman Catholic tradition, define it as theologically as "the relationship, in lived experience and reflective understanding (practice and theory), between the human spirit, individual and communal, and the divine spirit, or whatever is conceived . . . as ultimate in human and cosmic life." Then they add, "Spirituality is distinctively Christian when this relationship is conceived as mediated through the one Mediator, Jesus Christ, and when the divine spirit is understood as the Holy Spirit, poured forth by Father and Son into the heart of each believer, the church, the whole of humankind, and the whole creation."[4]

In the Anabaptist tradition there has been a lingering suspicion that too much emphasis on spirituality might encourage an affected piety without ethical obedience. Perhaps as a corrective to this ethical emphasis, Mennonites included an article on "Christian Spirituality" in their 1995 Confession of Faith. The confession describes spirituality as the "inner" transcendent relationship to God, the Spirit, which empowers and motivates our "outer" behavior. Spirituality is viewed as the dynamic of discipleship that is described as the "fruit of the Spirit" (Gal 5:22). The article warns that spirituality should not be separated from ethics and action. Thus we may speak of a *spirituality of discipleship.*[5]

This emphasis on ethics and action is by no means a repudiation of or contrast to a spirituality of grace. Grace is the source of motivation and enabling. Further, grace characterizes the attitude and mode of action. Discipleship is "faith active in love" in grateful response to God's gracious calling. The emphasis on discipleship in contrast to "belief" calls attention to the statement of James that faith without works is dead (2:17), or to Paul's assertion that ultimately our spirituality will be judged by our works (Rom 2:6-11), or to Jesus' statement that our response to grace is certified in our acts of genuine compassion (Mt 25:34-40).

The spiritual dimension is not merely one distinct aspect of our work. It is the transcendent dynamic expressed in all that we do. It is expressed in the basic assumptions and definitions that undergird our work, in the motivation that energizes our work, in the definition of mission that determines our goals and guides our strategies, in the relationships and communication that characterize our everyday work, and in the transformation we see taking place in our own lives and those we attempt to serve.

So we are speaking of spirituality as a kind of ethos, attitude, perspective or style. It encompasses the basic operating values and attitudes that characterize and give a transcendent dimension to our work. In this mode Walter Wink speaks of a "capitalist spirituality," while liberation theologians speak of a "spirituality of liberation" (Segundo Galilea). We might also speak of a spirituality of servanthood and of the first beatitude. One thinks of Paul's beautiful phrase "ourselves . . . your servants for Jesus' sake" (2 Cor 4:5 NIV).

Patterns of Spirituality

There are different spiritual systems, such as mysticism (Hinduism), humanism (Buddhist, Western individualist) and personal theism (Jewish, Muslim, Christian), and each has its own style. While it is dangerous to generalize too broadly, each system has its distinctive ambience. For example, while Christian mysticism has some things in common with Hindu and Buddhist mysticism, it has a distinct rationale and ethical character which can lead to quite different human relationships and responses to need. Aloysius Pieris points out that Christian humanism based on *agape* is quite different in its theological rationale and style from Buddhist humanism based on gnosis (knowledge).[6] And these basic differences elicit a different spiritual and ethical responses.

As background for our consideration of Christian spirituality, it may be helpful to review the general characterizations of some major spiritual systems. Hinduism, one of the oldest, is many-faceted, but it is held together by a deep mystical sense of the unity of the divine and human and of a karmic order to the universe. Karma is in the strictest sense a fate or destiny that is determined by previous lives in the cycle of reincarnation. Thus a *karmic spirituality* justifies things as they are and urges acceptance and conformity. Historically Hindu spirituality has down-played the significance of historical existence and has damp-ened urges toward social ethical responsibility and reform.

Buddhism began as a reform of Hindu polytheism and developed its own *humanistic spirituality.* Its relation to Hinduism is somewhat parallel to Protestantism's relation to Roman Catholicism. In the intervening millennia it has developed into many diverse religious patterns similar to Hinduism's. In Buddhism's original form it focused respon-sibility for one's individual condition on oneself. In the words of the Buddha, "I teach only two things: the cause of human sorrow and the way to become free from it."

Buddhism has developed an ascetic and gnostic spiritual-ity that stresses self-discipline and compliance with things-as-they-are. The spiritual goal is enlightenment. Ultimate enlightenment is the self-realization that individual histori-cal existence is merely a blip on the cosmic computer screen, a wave on the cosmic ocean. The enlightened one achieves *nirvana,* or reunification with the whole. This reunion and bliss is salvation. While Amidha Buddhism views the Buddha as a savior (bodhisattva) and some modern Buddhist sects have taken a commendable interest in hu-manitarian and peace work, such spirituality is not integral to the movement. Peace in this tradition means the eradica-tion of desire, which is the root of suffering. It has a counte-nance quite different from biblical shalom, which incorpo-rates social well-being and justice.

Jewish and Islamic religions have developed a much more formalistic spirituality based on divine law (Torah or Sharia). Indeed, one of Muslim scholars' major criticisms of Christianity is that it has no clearly prescribed legislation to define moral and religious practice. Muslim and Jewish spirituality focuses on strict obedience to divinely established patterns of behavior. Like Christianity, Judaism and Islam have produced their mystics, but mysticism does not characterize the general spiritual pattern of these religions.

All of these spiritual systems understand religion as a cultural product and adapt naturally to a *tribal* or *civic spirituality*. But Shintoism and, to some extent, Confucianism are civic spiritual systems by basic definition and character. (When Robert Bellah defined American "civil religion" and its demands on the individual, he extrapolated from the patterns of the civil religion of Japan.)[7] In anthropological terminology, they are totemic systems. Shintoism, for example, is very tolerant of different religious expressions but demands civic conformity to its myth of the divine nation.

Such descriptions of diverse systems could be listed indefinitely, but perhaps I have established the basic point that all spiritualities are not of the same genre. At the same time, we must be aware that there are many similar and overlapping patterns within these systems. This is important for those who are engaged in crosscultural service and confront a religious ethos at the popular level. There is a kind of human substratum of common religiosity, whether the cultural pattern be predominantly Buddhist, Islamic, Jewish or Christian. Nevertheless, the dominant cultural spirituality often dictates different ethical responses even when the religious patterns seem similar.

Distinctive Christian Spirituality
In this essay we are exploring the dimensions of Christian spirituality in which a personal Creator-God is related to us as a Savior, dynamic guide and enabler. Since this broad definition could also apply to Jewish or Muslim spirituality, we need to note the distinctive characteristics of Christian spirituality more precisely. Every Christian theological tra-

dition has its own list of characteristics and priorities. While the following list is broadly evangelical, it reflects the Anabaptist/Mennonite historical experience—its focus on Jesus, its history of persecution, its crosscultural experiences in mission and its perspective on the Bible. From this perspective, seven characteristics are essential.

1. Christian spirituality begins with a *profound sense of grace*. The first beatitude of Jesus, which comprehends all the rest, is "Blessed are those who know they are poor" (NEB). Jesus is prophet and teacher-example, but before that he is Savior-friend. He is God's vicarious initiative. Thus Christian service begins in gratitude to God for his gracious calling and enabling, which gives meaning and fulfillment to our lives. As Paul says, Christian missioners know themselves to be debtors to all humankind because of the grace they have received (Rom 1:4).

2. This sense of unearned blessing received as gift is the root of a *spirit of compassion* that identifies with all the needy. Such compassion is more than mercy or pity. It is more than an altruism which shares, perhaps out of pity, from self-justified affluence. Compassion (from Latin, meaning "suffering *with*") means feeling with, empathy, identification, experiencing life from the perspective of the impoverished. Roman Catholic writers speak of this as "a preferential option for the poor." This is not to say that there are no compassionate people in other religions, but only that compassion is essential to Christian spirituality and grows out of a sense of grace rather than achievement.

3. Christian spirituality is marked by *discipleship to the nonviolent Jesus*. This, as Wink points out, places one in direct opposition to the "domination system" of the world, which operates under the assumption that "redemptive violence" is the way of peace and justice. Wink translates

"Blessed are the meek" as "Blessed are the nonviolent for they shall inherit the earth."[8] As Menno Simons, the sixteenth-century Anabaptist leader, knew well, the call to discipleship is a call to take up the cross, to be sent out into the world as "lambs in the midst of wolves."

In our modern Western culture, discipleship is often misunderstood as simply following the moral example of Jesus. But in the biblical culture, discipleship indicated a close and continuing relationship. We moderns call learners "students," and the goal of learning is to become independent of and even to excel the teacher. But a disciple of Jesus never becomes independent of the teacher. A disciple is an *intern* or *apprentice* who seeks to absorb and reflect the character and skill of the master. For us Jesus is "the Master." We remain disciple-apostles, or servant-representatives, of Christ; and his Spirit is the enabling guide who remains in charge of the mission on which we have been sent. Thus a discipleship spirituality is characterized not only by commitment to follow Jesus' example but also by constant dependence on the Master.

Barbara Hendricks and Thomas Clarke describe this kind of disciple internship well.

Learning to relate to God, to oneself, to other persons, and to society, with both the tender compassion and the firm justice inherent in the gospel, is a whole way of life whose paradigm is the story of Jesus, Lamb of God and Lion of Judah, Servant of Yahweh who does not break the crushed reed or quench the wavering flame, but who will not waver or be crushed until true justice is established on earth (Isa. 42:3-4).[9]

4. Christian spirituality emphasizes *praxis*—action in obedience to Jesus Christ as Lord—rather than *doxis,* intellectual or mystical piety (Mt 7:21-23). Jesus' parable of the good

Samaritan contrasts the compassionate action of the Samaritan to the orthodox piety of the priest and Levite. In David Bosch's seminal work *A Spirituality of the Road,* he quotes Kosuke Koyama as saying, "It is better to be merciful in the name of Buddha than to be cruel in the name of Christ. It is better to become a neighbor with a Samaritan theology than . . . to desert the beaten victim with a Jewish theology."[10]

5. At the heart of Christian spirituality is the concept of *gospel,* or evangel. Thus we might call it a spirituality of evangelical servanthood. The impulse to universality and mission is implicit in and intrinsic to Christian spirituality. Service is not merely a good work. Servanthood and sharing the good news of the new possibility in Christ are at its very center.

6. Christian spirituality lives in and is nurtured by a *community of believers.* It is inherently a social spirituality. Its metaphors are social and political—a kingdom, a colony, a people of God. Its ethics are instinctively social and other-directed—honor and respect for each other, responsibility and integrity in relationships, serving each other in love. It is a spirituality of *koinonia,* or community.

7. In summary, Christian spirituality is a spirituality of *agape* based on Jesus' paradigm of incarnation. The Beatitudes are a good description of this new paradigm. It is a spirituality of cross and resurrection, not crusade and conquest. In *Waterbuffalo Theology* Kosuke Koyama calls missionaries to renounce a crusading mentality and adopt a crucified mind.[11]

Spiritual Formation

Spiritual formation means being formed into the image of Christ through sharing his sufferings (Phil 3:10). The apostle Paul also describes the formation of the Christian attitude as suffering, perseverance, character and hope grounded in the love of God which is poured into our hearts (Rom 5:3-5). All this, he explains, is the experience of life as a continual gift of grace and enabling, which gives our work an air of joy. The sixteenth-century Anabaptist martyrs called such formation *Nachfolge Christi*, or discipleship.

Discipleship and spiritual formation are not two different processes. The so-called spiritual disciplines are of value for spiritual training when they are set within a life of committed action. The end of the disciplines is not a spiritual experience in itself. Meister Eckhart, the great medieval mystic, insisted that his monks should never hesitate to break their meditation and prayers to serve the needs of a beggar at the door.

As in so many other aspects of spirituality, our dualistic views of spiritual reality as separate and superior to the social and material have prompted us to regard spiritual disciplines as ends in themselves. Discipleship is understood as an inward "spiritual" (mystical) relationship, detached from active following in the vocations of life.

Spiritual formation is not simply a matter of retreating to a place of solitude for prayer, Scripture study and self-denial in order to be more spiritual. Of course, like sleep and relaxed times for physical nourishment, such sanctuary is indispensable; but Jesus' withdrawals to "rest" took place in the midst of a frantic schedule of active service and teaching. According to Jesus, the only way to know God (spirituality) is to be obedient to his will (discipleship), and at the heart of discipleship is love of one's neighbor.[12]

Spiritual formation must also include a rigorous element of nonconformity to the spirit of the age (Rom 12:1-2). Our cultural formation has warped our outlook on life. Hendricks and Clarke call it "cultural deformation." Thus spiritual discipline must include critical evaluation and "deconstruction" of the secular culture that has formed us. The caution of Hendricks and Clarke is worth quoting:

> Too often the language of religious and spiritual formation tends to become bland and abstract. In contrast, mission bearers in the twenty-first century from technologically developed countries such as the United States must in their spiritual formation counteract the powerful cultural *deformation* affecting potential future missionaries. When this is done, then formation is understood in continuity with the biblical, and specifically the Pauline, themes of *re*formation, *con*formation, and *trans*formation.[13]

This aspect of spiritual formation is of critical importance for one who would serve Christ in a crosscultural vocation. A spirituality of "nonconformity to this world" in this context requires an intentional repudiation of the competitive, consumer-oriented, individualistic, confrontational spirit that has permeated much of our goal-oriented, Western service and evangelism. Jesus' teaching and example of service and servanthood must be taken with utmost seriousness.

Special Marks of a Missionary Spirituality

For those who have a special calling to be representatives of the God-movement—to be catalytic agents of peace and justice—a number of spiritual qualities are essential. We might well begin with an observation by Michael Reilly:

> The missionary is one whose interior life is oriented to non-believers, to those who do not profess faith in Jesus Christ. It is this orientation which determines his life style and spirituality. . . . The missionary is one who intends . . . to bring all people to explicit awareness of God's loving

plan for them, and one who works to establish the goals of God's Mission of *shalom* so that humankind may both enjoy them and praise their source.[14]

Such an orientation implies and requires a deep respect for those who differ from us—respect for both the persons and their cultures. The old militant attitude that viewed the pagan cultures and their representatives as the demonic enemy is totally inappropriate. For Jesus it was not Judaism or Hellenism that was the enemy, but "Satan," the spiritual foe of all humanity. The "enemy" is a common opponent and despoiler of both the servant-evangelists and those they are attempting to evangelize. In any case, if those whom we try to serve become hostile, we are commanded to love our enemies.

Further, respect implies appreciation for the values of other cultures and willingness to contextualize the expression of Christian spirituality. For example, Lynn Samaan details some Muslim concepts of holiness that are quite commensurate with Christian ideals, such as "humility, regular prayer life, fasting, alms giving and concern for the poor; a life of sacrifice and suffering; a power to heal, deliver from demons (jinns) and miracles; memorization and meditation on the Word of God." Then she adds, "A Christian called to work among an Islamic people has a responsibility to carefully learn the forms of spirituality and then diligently adjust to these forms as daily habits of life and worship."

Samaan observes, "Protestant Christian missionaries have often failed to identify spiritually with the various peoples and cultures, and as a result failed to incarnate the gospel for them in a manner the local people understand. Instead of representing holiness, they often represent materialism, immorality, pride, arrogance, insensitivity, and secularism."[15]

Christian service is a reciprocal and mutual activity. It is not something that the strong and mature do to and for the weak and ignorant. To be authentically Christian, service must be a mutual experience of development and transformation. The service experience is a formative part of the worker's spiritual development. And this is inevitably, indeed necessarily, a reciprocal spiritual development involving receiving as well as giving.

We might speak of this as a dialogical relationship involving listening and responding. For service workers this dialogue is seldom academic. Rather, they must enter into the religious culture of the poor and engage them at a very personal level. At this level one does not so much discuss ideas as share aspirations, hopes and fears, and one's response will grow directly out of one's spirituality, whatever its depth or shallowness. To be authentically Christian, such a dialogical relation requires a counterpoint spirituality in which the melody of the gospel intertwines with the melodies of culture.

Bosch provides us with another helpful reminder:

In 2 Corinthians, however, Paul argues that true Christian spirituality is not to be found in the superhuman and the miraculous, but in the commonplace. Our problem is that we have even turned the commonplaces of the gospel into something romantic and folksy. We have provided the cross with a halo and changed the stable of Bethlehem into something idyllic and sentimental. This view misses the terribly mundane and ordinary nature of these images. Likewise, the criteria for missionary service and spirituality are not in magnificent and romantic accomplishments, but in ordinary daily existence. So Paul opposes the impressive arsenal of his opponents with down-to-earth weapons: patience, truth, love, weakness, service, modesty and respect. Under no circumstances should people be bulldozed with the gospel, for it ceases to be the gospel when foisted upon people. It is possible to be unaggressive and missionary at the same time. It is, indeed, the only way of being truly missionary.[16]

6

Conversion
& Social
Transformation
"Engaging the Powers"

●●●

*M*ODERN THEOLOGICAL LIBERALISM HAS BEEN OPTIMISTIC
about the possibility of reforming socioeconomic systems by
rational means. Similarly, it has been optimistic about the
freedom of individuals to determine their own destiny. Liberals were confident that the universe is ruled by divine
reason and that human rationality reflects that divinity.
Working in cooperation with the laws of reason, human
beings could make real progress toward social, economic
and political equity and justice. Even after the decline of
theological liberalism following World War II, economic and
political liberals perpetuated this optimism in their development schemes to raise the status of the "less-developed"
nations, referred to as the "Third World."

Diminished Confidence
But the cultural mood of the 1960s and 1970s was changing.

The overconfidence of the United States in its ability to manage the world was shaken by events like John F. Kennedy's failed attempt to invade Cuba at the Bay of Pigs and the Vietnam fiasco. In the 1960s President Lyndon Johnson's attempt to remedy the growing poverty in the United States by spending large amounts of federal money in his "War on Poverty" produced results far more meager than what had been hoped for. The disappointing results of international development schemes led to a loss of confidence in political and economic systems to control and manage world affairs. In the late 1970s the oil crisis, which ended with poor nations owing impossibly large debts at high interest rates, exacerbated liberals' loss of confidence.

Management of the sociopolitical order was proving far more complicated and intractable than had been expected. The rational laws of nature did not seem to operate smoothly in the social order. I remember my major professor in graduate school, himself an erstwhile liberal, introducing the word *surd* into our vocabulary. There is a mysterious irrational element in the cosmic machine, he said. There are frustrating constraints on individual efforts. There seems to be a self-defeating element in even our best-intentioned and most scientific schemes for resolving human problems. This has come to be called "the law of unintended effects." In the words of Robert Burns, "The best laid schemes o' mice an' men gang aft agley!"

This loss of confidence in institutions is also reflected in attitudes toward the institutional church and its programs. Since the mid-1960s we have seen a steady decline in the global programs of both the ecumenical movement and mainline churches.

In theology, thinkers like Karl Barth and Emil Brunner in Europe and Reinhold Niebuhr and John Bennett in the

United States were challenging liberal optimism already in the 1930s and 1940s. They were making a much more sober assessments of the human situation. Niebuhr spoke of "moral man and immoral society" and favored a realistic politics of power rather than rational idealism. In the late 1960s William Stringfellow, a lawyer and lay theologian, analyzed the social crisis in apocalyptic terms of approaching judgment and imminent disaster. He spoke of the demonic powers dominating human beings and ruling society by the threat of death. Paul Ricoeur, a French scholar, wrote about "the symbolism of evil." And both theologians and biblical scholars began to reexamine the New Testament teaching about the "principalities and powers," which Paul said rule this age (see Eph 3:10; Col 2:15).

Optimistic visions for the development of "backward" nations were fueled in part by naive assumptions about the innate goodness and rationality of the human heart. When a critic suggested that Niebuhr's phrase "moral man and immoral society" might better read "immoral man and worse society," Niebuhr agreed.

In part the problem stemmed from an oversimplification of the complexity of social systems and an unwarranted faith in the individual's ability to triumph over the system. At midcentury we were not yet so aware of the "system" and "systemic violence." The civil rights movement helped rivet such concepts in our minds. We began to be aware that racism is more than the simple accumulation of individual prejudice. It is a self-fulfilling presumption that governs social institutions and conditions individuals. Thus it feeds upon itself.

Further, the problem stemmed in part from the secularist assumption that religious belief itself was part of the problem, certainly not part of the solution. This secular disdain for spiritual dimensions in the analysis and cure of the world's social problems tempted developers into overconfidence. Unfortunately, as Charles Elliott points out in his *Comfortable Compassion? Poverty, Power and the Church,* the churches bought into this secular vision far too readily.[1]

Principalities and Powers

More recently, though beginning already in the 1960s, theologians began to recognize that the biblical picture of "principalities and powers" offers a more realistic assessment of the nature of the social order. I am not talking about the Pentecostal/charismatic revival of concern with demons and view of missions as a war against the demonic legions of darkness. The biblical picture is far more sophisticated than that! My point has to do with the recognition that there are spiritual authorities and powers—which secular analysts call social, ideological, systemic, institutional—that control human cultures. The theological task has been to understand the sociospiritual nature of these powers and how they fit into God's intended order for the world.

Are the principalities and powers inherently evil, or are they created orders gone wrong? Are they detached spiritual personalities that affect the fallen human mind? Are they projections of the human subconscious? Are they to be identified with the institutional empires that dominate the lives of individuals? Or are they the personification of ideologies, myths and rationalizations that sanction the self-centered systems that control society? However they are conceptualized, there is little doubt about their clout in world affairs.

We cannot explore all of these questions, but several observations are pertinent to our topic. The New Testament uses a variety of terms to describe this phenomenon—"powers," "authorities," "rulers of this age," "elemental spirits," "angels," "demons." This in itself suggests that we are not dealing with a simple phenomenon. Modern words like *office* (such as the office of sheriff), *system, spirit* (as in spirit of a meeting or of a mob), *institution, ideology, religion* and *tradition* seem to translate the idea. These represent the authorities that provide the rationale, culture and powers that control life in society.

"Authorities" become institutionalized and harden into "traditions," which in turn condition the self-definition of individuals. We encounter them in the slogans, symbols and organizations of society. They define and dictate the spiritual (as defined earlier) mode of cultural patterns and relationships. They define justice, wisdom, social values, the meaning of "human," the status and roles of individuals in society and so on. They provide rationalization for the social order. Concepts like karma, *dukkha* (suffering), chance or fate, private property, self-defense, free trade and individual rights have conditioned whole civilizations!

The powers dominate through a system that controls and constrains the possibilities of individuals. Walter Wink calls it the "Domination System." Although this system has its origins in human society, it is not completely under the control and management of human individuals. It takes on a life, identity, goals and dynamic of its own, and in a kind of Frankensteinian reflex it conditions the definitions, values, assumptions, social classifications and myths with which a culture operates. David Bakan, whom Wink quotes, characterizes the satanic character of these powers that rule world systems as "self-assertion, self-protection and self-expression; the formation of separations, isolation, alienation; the repression of thought, feeling, and impulse."[2] This self-centered core is at the center of all human social and political systems.

Two more things need to be said about these powers. First, they are not essentially evil or demonic. God did not create them as demonic divinities. They were created by God as part of the human reality. They are creaturely—that is, they are limited in their ability to achieve their goals. They are subject to what sociologists call "the law of unintended consequences." And in their arrogance they are caught in the frustration of self-contradiction. This is the human condition that theologians refer to as "fallen."

The institutional systems, which are the concrete manifestation of the powers, are of human origin and embody the spirit of a society. Thus their demonic expression is actually a reflection of human idolatry, autonomy and self-centeredness. Paul says in Colossians that all these "thrones," "dominions," "rulers" or "powers" were created by Christ and for him (1:16). But they have become perverted and alienated (fallen) through their idolatrous self-centeredness. And the results of their idolatry are anarchy, dehumanization, violence and death.

Second, as their Creator and Redeemer, Jesus Christ is their Lord. Through the cross he has "disarmed the rulers and authorities" and exposed their aberration (Col 2:15). And Ephesians 3:10 says that God intends for the church to make that lordship known to these "rulers and authorities in the heavenly places." So the principalities and powers are redeemable, and the church has a mandate to make known God's original intention for them. This is the basis for the church's intervention in the social, political and economic aspects of culture. But note carefully that it is an intervention characterized by the cross and God's power of resurrection.

Consider the phenomenon of poverty. Poverty is not simply the lack of material wealth. In that respect *poverty* is a relative term. Many affluent people suffer from real poverty of spirit, and the relatively poor are often rich in human character. Thus poverty is not caused or cured simply by the supply of material goods or money. It is a complex social condition which is the product of human characteristics such as anxiety, greed, apathy, injustice and will to power.

Poverty can be fully understood only as a dehumanizing social syndrome where the poor have internalized the values of and adapted to the violence of an unjust system (the "powers"). It is a cultural network of codependence in which the poor see themselves as "nobodies," "second-class citizens," "failures" who are somehow guilty and deserving of their fate (karma). Wink tells of a South American peasant woman who was surprised to find out that the Bible nowhere said that she had to suffer![3]

So we have a system that has been manipulated by the powerful for their own self-serving advantage and internalized by the weak for their own survival. The ultimate sanction for the system is the fear of deprivation and death. The rich fear the poor masses who want what they have, and the impoverished masses fear the physical violence, humiliation and loss of life that the powerful can inflict. All this is institutionalized into an ideology that rationalizes poverty and a legal system that enforces the socioeconomic order. This is a rough sketch of the complexity of the inner workings of the "Domination System," or in biblical terms, the "principalities and powers," as they have been perverted through idolatrous self-interest.

The Need for Radical Conversion
Charles Elliott explains how inadequate the secular presuppositions and models of development are to deal with this

kind of situation and how difficult it is for churches to confront the system with the radicalness of the gospel. At the end of chapter eight of *Comfortable Compassion?* Elliott comes to what he calls the core of his argument:

What I have tried to show, both in analysis and anecdote, is that the Churches have over-invested in approaches to development that are not necessarily destructive or unnecessary, but which are inadequate by themselves and which are very easily subverted into countersigns [of the Kingdom of God]. The school becomes a school for the elite. The agricultural project becomes an agricultural project for the successful, progressive farmer. The hospital becomes a disease palace. The Church development office becomes another middle-class, top-down bureaucracy. That is not to deny that they do a perfectly respectable job and a job that perhaps has to be done. It is, however, to call in question whether that is the real vocation of the Church, and whether it is likely to produce an authentic pattern of development which fully reflects biblical understandings of the nature of man and of society.[4]

Elliott contends that the real basis for inequalities in the world lies in human nature and not in economic systems. Wink quotes liberation theologian Domingos Barbe as saying that the sickness of our world is a spiritual illness that comes from a lack of a living relationship with God, and Wink adds, "God must supplant the upstart ego. People do need to be 'reborn' from their primary socialization in an alienated and alienating system."[5] Václav Havel writes, "A better system will not automatically ensure a better life. In fact the opposite is true: only by creating a better life can a better system be developed."[6]

We cannot assume that appropriate technology and small

entrepreneurial projects will result in the kingdom of God, that is, the kind of interdependent community that Jesus advocated. When, for example, we help impoverished farmers onto the economic escalator with a loan or appropriate technology, we are inducting them into the system—a system of greedy profit making. Whether the individual is greedy or not, the superhuman powers that inform and control the system exercise constraints and define success or failure. Social transformation requires change in both the system and the individual. So long as the entrepreneurial project stays small, we can control the effects to some degree, but unless the farmer has been resocialized in the kingdom of God, there is little or no chance of significant systemic change.

Therefore Elliott concludes that the mission of the church is "the creation of an alternative consciousness, which in the spirit of the magnificat and beatitudes puts the poor and the powerless at its centre." He explains:

This alternative consciousness is not paternalistic or condescending: it is a consciousness that turns upside down the priorities and assumptions of twentieth century industrialized, secularized acquisitiveness (whether capitalist or socialist) and judges relationships, structures, and economic ties not by what profit it brings to the dominant partner but by how much it enlarges the life chances of the subordinate partner. . . . The rich and powerful, in other words, have to learn to use their wealth and power not for their own aggrandizement, but for the goals set by the poor and powerless.[7]

This is precisely what the New Testament calls *metanoia* and *epistrephō*. *Metanoia,* which is usually translated "repentance," means reorientation or the adoption of a new attitude. *Epistrephō,* usually translated "conversion," places emphasis on this change as a return to God's original intention. This is the gospel meaning of revolution.

We must also emphasize that the poor as well as the rich must be converted. The poor have internalized the values and adapted to the violence of an unjust system. They aspire to be rich and self-sufficient. The only option they see is to use the system to beat the system. They identify the way of individual initiative and competition, rather than interdependence, as the way to achieve this individualized goal. They see salvation as an escape from the system rather than a radical conversion of the system.

In 1991 a small group of us toured a Mennonite Central Committee coconut project in Bangladesh. It was an excellent example of an entrepreneurial job-creation project, which gave some fifty women and men a chance to improve their economic situation. After we had toured the various processes, all the workers gathered to have their pictures taken with the visitors. Then as we were ready to get into the car and leave, the Bangladeshi women gathered around the American women in our group with outstretched hands, begging, "Take me with you."

While we may have great sympathy for these women who daily live so near the survival line, this mindset must be changed if their situation is to be improved. But before we too quickly fault the project, the workers or the international staff, we must look at ourselves. It is *our* affluent, consumer lifestyle that they emulate. It is our too-easy compliance with an unjust international economic system that exacerbates their poverty. How can we expect such impoverished people to take our words seriously when our examples are so contradictory?

Characteristics of a Program for Transformation
Gustavo Gutiérrez has said, "The core of human and social

transformation is spiritual. Without the change in attitudes and behavior implicit in *metanoia* (conversion), humans remain self-centered creatures. Sin, both individual and institutionalized, is a basic deterrent to social transformation. Sin has been defined as the 'social and cosmic anti-creation' resulting in injustice and exploitation; racism and oppression; alienation and anomie."[8]

In a contribution to the Wheaton conference "Evangelism and Social Responsibility" (1982), Wayne Bragg offered a "transformation" model that goes "beyond development." Transformation, he said, aims to (1) enable persons to become fully human; (2) change social and economic principles to conform to the Kingdom principles of peace, justice, and love manifested in the community of God; (3) transform both the material and spiritual dimensions of life as a joint enterprise between God and man. He summarized the characteristics of such a transformation as "(1) providing life-sustenance, (2) equity, (3) justice, (4) dignity and self worth, (5) freedom, (6) participation, (7) reciprocity, (8) ecological soundness, (9) hope, (10) spiritual transformation."[9]

This description of social transformation attempts to gather up the individual-personal, the social and the spiritual into a holistic model. It views the "kingdom" as a social and not simply a religious reality, and this certainly implies that the transformation process is spiritual in character. Bringing social and economic structures into conformity with kingdom principles of peace, justice and love is precisely a spiritual goal. But Bragg's summary list still shows signs of the old evangelistic-social service dualism. It enumerates the characteristics as though the spiritual were a separate item on the development agenda (number 10).

Here we may return to my earlier metaphor of the Amazon River with its many tributaries intermingling as they flow into one stream. Setting all these dimensions of our life in the perspective of a covenant relationship between God and the human community is the task of spiritual transformation. Even the most mundane, earthy tasks of aid must be suffused with spiritual power. From the human side, this means doing the task "wholeheartedly and as a service to the Lord" (paraphrase of Col 3:22). And from the divine side, our work must be infused with the spirit/Spirit of Christ, and empowered by him.

What would be some characteristics of a program of intervention aimed at this kind of transformation? Focus on the spiritual dimension of our work will affect our understanding of service—our program priorities and our way of operating. It is not enough to simply add a spiritual component to our otherwise secular program. I suggest the following.

First, an approach *patterned after the example of Christ,* willingly making itself vulnerable in the offer of conciliatory service, is essential (Phil 2:6-11). Christ is the pattern of *agape*-love, not some principle of self-abnegation. Agapaic service is service of Christ in our fellow human beings. It does not hesitate to take the towel to wash others' feet, or if necessary to die for them.

Such agapaic service is also referred to as service "in the name of Jesus." The first disciples insisted that the miraculous outcomes of their ministry were due to "the name of Jesus." This is not a simple religious shibboleth, and we need constantly to remind ourselves of its meaning. When the first disciples invoked the name of Jesus for healing and reconciling, they were recognizing that the deed was done by his power and command and according to his spirit of compassion (see "Presence as Parousia" in chapter two). They were expressing their own sense of the Master's mandate—as Paul

put it, "ourselves as your servants for Jesus' sake" (2 Cor
4:5).

Such service in the name of Christ calls for the spiritual
gift of tactful discrimination. Jesus did not always give people
what they wanted or thought they needed (Jn 6:26-27) but
pointed them to their true need. We dare not presume that
everyone who asks for "bread" is also interested in "transformation." While we supply bread, we also attempt to
awaken spiritual awareness that recognizes responsibility
for the neighbor. In following Jesus' example we must be
true, on the one hand, to our own deepest experience of
grace and our understanding of the real needs of those we
serve. On the other hand, as servants we must not dictate
the terms of our service.

Second, this discriminatory imperative in transformational ministry makes an *incarnational* approach essential.
Servanthood includes solidarity with and dependence on
those we attempt to serve. Here we should note that in the
first instance "incarnation" meant change for the intervening agent. "The Word became flesh and lived among us" (Jn
1:14). We dare not impose the details of cultural response
from an outside cultural perspective. The pattern of transformation should be an intrinsic response to agapaic identification.

Of course, a full-blown incarnation in a foreign culture is
impossible in the few brief years of a service assignment. But
we can take an empathic and compassionate stance. We can
identify with and try to see the situation from the perspective of those we serve.

I have tried many times without overwhelming success to
put into words what an incarnational or solidarity stance
might involve. It means accepting the distinguishing characteristics of the culture in which we serve as the limiting

context for work. Jesus operated very self-consciously as a first-century Jew. Of course he broke through some of the cultural barriers this imposed on him, but he lived, ministered and died as a Jew. Indeed, some of his Jewish attitudes and actions give us a twinge of embarrassment. We try to soften his rebuke to the Canaanite woman who in faith pled with him to heal her daughter. When she knelt before him with the simple request, "Lord, help me!" he replied, "It is not right to take the children's food and toss it to the dogs" (Mt 15:25-26). Her faith created the point of breakthrough, but Jesus clearly operated from within Jewish cultural assumptions.

It means, further, that we take the culture seriously and learn to know its values from the inside. Where critical appraisal of a cultural practice may be necessary—and all cultures have such practices—it must be based on a deep respect for the culture and its people. Respect for a culture also implies that patterns or ideas being proposed from the outside will be contextualized, or inculturated. The freedom to make such contextualizations is spoken of in the New Testament as the freedom from legalism. It is the Holy Spirit of Christ that guides in the transformation of cultures after the pattern of Jesus, and not a legalistic application of literal texts.

Yet another aspect is genuine dependence on and appreciation of the hosts' hospitality and sustaining support. Genuine interdependence is fundamental in a spiritual approach to social and material services. Listening, learning and willingness to adapt to cultural styles are essential. "Partnering" and "walking alongside" are expressions of this characteristic.

Furthermore, an incarnational approach will make penetration of the culture with the spirit of Christ the aim of the mission, not simply the rescue of individuals from it. As much as possible one does not attempt to impose or substitute one's own modern culture or religious ideology, but to introduce Jesus and his way of life. We seek to incarnate the Spirit/spirit of Jesus. The question is how Jesus would address the culture.

A third characteristic of transformational intervention is an *integrated, holistic* approach based on our understanding of the essentially spiritual nature of human beings. This implies a social, community development approach in which verbal ministries (witness, counseling, teaching) and peacemaking are integral. And presupposing, as I do, that the program is Christian, the witness is to Christ as the source and dynamic of authentic human life and relationship. Jobs creation and economic development, emergency relief, conciliation and conflict resolution ministries, and medical programs should all be carried out in this contextual framework.

Fourth, transformative service will be *participatory.* It will actively include those being served in their own transformation.[10] This includes what Samuel Escobar has called a "eucharistic" approach, in which those who receive help are expected to voluntarily and generously share from the benefits they have received. Escobar is especially concerned that "the Christological sources of [our] compassion and spirit of service" continue to be shared in a chain reaction.

In her book *India, India,* Lisa Hobbs tells about a trip to a Maharastran village with Father Ferrer, who was director of the Roman Catholic Seva Mandal (Service Society). They were going to locate and dig a well in the village. But Father Ferrer saw it as more than a well-digging project. He saw it as starting "a quiet revolution there." He explained, "The Mandal means simply Society, and that is what we have formed to help the farmers—a cooperative society but with a difference. We don't want to just feed the people; we want to give them an understanding of all the forces that can change their lives."

When they arrived, Ferrer spoke to the villagers about our one humanity under the one God and of the responsibility such "brotherhood" lays upon us to freely share our wealth. Although he did not identify it as such, he asserted the basic gospel principle that in order to receive we must give. Then, rather than arbitrarily deciding which farmer should get the first well, he engaged one farmer in a spirited public conversation that ended with the man promising to pay back the full loan, half of the first year's profits even though they would be small, and besides that to give one-third of his fifty acres of land so that others could live—and to do all this voluntarily and in good grace. Only then did Ferrer agree to locate the well on the farmer's property.

The decision made, he encouraged the man: "You are frightened. Remember. When you give you become rich. And the more you give the richer you become. You do not believe, but truly it is surprising."[11] This is an excellent picture of participatory development!

Fifth and finally, in a transformational approach, service is defined as *empowerment*. In "The Anabaptist Vision," written in 1943, Harold Bender says, "Discipleship is a concept which meant the transformation of the entire way of life of individual believers and of society so that it should be fashioned after the teachings and example of Christ."[12] Surely the service ministries of the church fall under the mandate to make "disciples of all nations" (Mt 28:19-20).

A transformational intention and strategy must go beyond the merely ameliorative. It is more than giving emergency aid. It implies more than economic and technical development. The transformation of individuals-in-society requires a holistic sociospiritual approach to both individual and community development.

Unfortunately, the concept of discipleship has become disassociated from empowerment for life as children of God in human community. It has been identified, on the one hand, with "believing" a particular interpretation of the Jesus story and, on the other, with morals and ethical disciplines. Thus making disciples has been understood in the narrow terms of evangelism, that is, the winning of individual converts to belief in Jesus as a personal Savior and the formation of churches to teach these converts the ethical disciplines. But discipling is more than making individual converts to a Western religious message and style of church.

Transformational intervention in the name of Christ means more than "church planting," as that term has come to be applied. We are working for kingdom values and goals, not merely church (that is, religious) goals. While these may have a positive relationship, they are not the same. The church is not the kingdom; neither is it in control of the kingdom. The question is rather whether our church programs are effectively representing and promoting the kingdom of God. And on the field the question is whether the local churches with which we seek to cooperate are truly empowering people for life in God's kingdom. Where kingdom-oriented congregations are found, they can and should become the point of contact and the base for kingdom transformation.

Shalom
To put this in more biblical language, *shalom*—the inclusive word for salvation, justice and peace—is the goal of trans-

formation. Shalom, or peace, as a transformative ideal must be given a functional role in our various programs. In the words of Howard John Loewen, we must understand "peace as a transformational grammar."[13] The objective is to empower individuals and their societies to discover and live out "the gospel of peace" in all areas of life. This will require a more explicitly spiritual, in contrast to merely technical, dimension in our service programs.

If we seriously define our peace mandate as a mandate to transform and empower the weak and vulnerable, then we must consider the question how they are to be motivated. As the Peru Declaration stated, they must be motivated and enabled to be "agents of their own transformation." How do we energize them to "wash each other's feet"? This question is raised to a new level of importance.

A clue to the answer of this question comes from Jesus himself. Remember that his preaching of shalom and justice was mainly to the poor. How did he expect them to be motivated and energized to share, serve and bear each other's burdens? According to John 6, such empowerment would come through spiritual nourishment—from partaking in the body and blood of Christ, not from eating the physical bread that Jesus miraculously provided.

7

Relating to People of Other Faiths

··

*I*T SEEMS CLEAR THAT WE NEED A NEW PARADIGM FOR DEALING
with religion in the postmodern sociopolitical order. The
missionary movement of the nineteenth and twentieth centuries assumed the Enlightenment paradigm of "toleration"
for religion within an overarching secular order. In that
model the political society is to be secular, and morals are
to be regulated by empirical and pragmatic factors. Religion
is reduced to the private sector. Clearly, this model is under
attack both in the Western democracies and in traditional
religious states like India and Iran. The fall of secular com-
munism in the Soviet empire and the less dramatic, but fully
as significant, revisionist shift toward religious tolerance in
China, Cambodia and Vietnam signal the need for some
careful rethinking.

Christianity must find some approach other than that of
"culture wars"—that is, one "fundamentalism" versus an-

other. The older religious imperialism must become a thing of the past. On the other hand, toleration based on the secularizing of public culture also seems to be unsatisfactory as a long-term solution. Secular socialism proved a serious menace to religion itself. And secular individualism has posed a grave threat to social cohesion and morals. From the experience of Europe and America, it seems inevitable that secular interests cancel out public religious values in the long run. That is the meaning of the present Christian Right's political attempt to reestablish Christian values in America.

What might toleration based on mutual respect and cooperation among religious groups look like? We do not yet know how a genuinely pluralistic mix of religions in a single society would work; but it is clear that it would require a more cooperative, consensus model than the 51-percent-winner-take-all model we have championed in the United States. And how might the church give an authentic witness to the unique and universal revelation of God in Christ in such a political order? Would real pluralism rule out all competitive proselytizing? If both neutrality and imperialistic competition are out, what stance shall we take?

All of these questions cannot be solved in this brief chapter, but merely raising them frames the context in which we are asking the question of our relation to people of other faiths. First we will look at some of the basic theological presuppositions and definitions that underlie an approach to the questions. Then in a final section I will make a few practical suggestions based on these definitions.

Strategic Suggestions from the New Testament
Perhaps no world government has attempted a more pluralistic stance than ancient Rome with its pantheon of gods for the empire. And it was in this cultural climate that Christi-

anity was born. This suggests that we might get some strategic insight from the New Testament itself. How did the men and women of first-generation Christianity bear witness to Jesus as the Christ? What were their attitudes toward those of other religions? After examining the biblical material briefly for leads, I will suggest some theological ABCs that can give us direction.

We should note that the apostle Paul faced much the same kind of problem that we do today as he crossed ethnic cultures. He could not, indeed chose not to, go into the various cultures of west Asia without a clear religious identity. He was automatically identified with the culture religion of Judaism, just as we are identified with a cultural model of Christianity. But Paul refused to promote a Judaistic model of Christian faith.

The same tensions existed in the emerging Christian movement that we experience. There was a conservative group, of whom Peter was the moderate spokesman, who insisted on a literal transfer of religious and moral definitions and practices. For them such requirements were "biblical." Jesus himself had accepted them as the religious framework for his mission. Therefore they insisted that Gentiles who wished to follow Christ must accept at least the minimal requirements of Judaistic religion, which was the culture that had nurtured and defined the Christ.

While Paul himself was identified culturally as Jewish, he insisted that his hearers did not need to become Jewish in order to be followers of Christ. He refused to perpetuate the central cultural symbols of Jewish biblicism as a necessary expression of faith in Christ. He made the practice of circumcision peripheral, if not detrimental to faith, and he refused to honor the purity laws that separated Jews from Gentiles. He dealt contextually with the religious practices demanded of Gentile Christians by the Jerusalem Council (Acts 15:28-29; compare 1 Cor 8).

Paul taught that Christ has inaugurated a new reality that requires a radically new approach to cultural religions. Thus he could write to the Galatian Christians, "For in Christ Jesus neither circumcision nor uncircumcision counts for anything; the only thing that counts is faith working through love" (Gal 5:6; compare 1 Cor 7:19). One can quite properly paraphrase his restatement of this in Galatians 6:15 as "Neither Jewish religion nor non-Jewish religion counts for anything; what is all-important is transformation."[1]

Paul called both pagans and his Jewish compatriots to the same new social-spiritual reality. If we follow this biblical example, we will understand our mission not as proselytizing our listeners into cultural Christianity but as calling them to a new identity "in Christ"—an identity to be lived out in their own culture. For Paul this meant a new pattern of ethnic, economic, sexual and social relationships that obliterated the old cultural lines defined by religion (Gal 3:26-28).

Second, we should note Paul's attitude and approach to the various religions he confronted. He did not condemn pagan religions as demonic in their totality. He recognized the values and spiritual insights in some of their religious teachings and practices. On Mars Hill in Athens, for example, he commended his hearers for their religious devotion and identified his message with their image to an "unknown god" (Acts 17:22-31). He clearly acknowledged that the sincere virtues of pagans who keep the spirit of God's law are valid in God's sight. (This is clearly the presupposition of his argument in Romans 2:6-16.) Their virtues are not "splendid vices," as Augustine put it! Rather than condemning, Paul was concerned to point to the true source and authentic pattern of these values: the disclosure of God in Christ. He was particularly careful not to take credit to himself as a new religious guru (Acts 10:14-18). He was not attempting to found a "new religion."

Further, Paul taught that pagans will be judged by their actions ("works"), not by their relative knowledge of the Mosaic tradition. A new standard that transcends religious ideology and law has been put into place. And this new standard applies to everyone—Jews, Christians and pagans alike (Rom 2:4-7, 14-16). God, he says, is God of both Jews and Gentiles, and both will be saved by the same standard. The immediate contrast here is between legal observance of religious codes, in this case Mosaic codes, and "patiently doing good [in the pursuit of] glory and honor and immortality" (v. 7). The contrast to such persistence in authentic well-doing is self-seeking rejection of truth and following of evil (v. 8). Paul praises the former and says that they will be judged "according to my gospel . . . through Christ Jesus" (v. 16).

This is a crucial text! Since the time of the Reformation, evangelical Protestant thought has contrasted works and faith, appealing to Paul in contrast to James as the champion of faith. Especially in post-Reformation orthodoxy, which has greatly influenced current evangelical thought, faith came to be equated with belief in orthodox doctrine. But in chapter 3 of Romans it becomes clear that Paul is identifying faith with the secret longing and action for righteousness which only the Christ can judge. Here in 3:28-30 he contrasts "faith" with legal observance, and he says that both Jews and Gentiles will be saved/justified by faith. All humankind will be justified "by faith," not by observance of religious codes, either Mosaic or pagan. And now, after two thousand years of institutional religious developments, we must add "Christian" codes! What counts is a sincere will to do God's will. That is the measure of "faith."

Clearly Paul is not teaching salvation by works, but rather that honoring God's law is a demonstration and validation of saving faith. If salvation were by works, that is, proper religious observance, then one would have to determine what is the proper religion. That, of course, is precisely what the Jewish proselytizers were doing. They were converting Gentiles to Judaism and its "works." Paul by contrast teaches that where the law of God is sincerely being honored, even in relative ignorance, there one can presume the presence of faith. This implies a positive rather than a critical or disparaging approach to other religious cultures.

The risen Christ establishes a new criterion by which to evaluate religious cultures. They are not subject to the relativities of any other religious culture. Rather, they are under the judgment of the God who has made himself known in Christ. While this may give the biblical religions some historical tactical advantage, Paul writes, it does not mean that they are God's favorites (Rom 3:1-2). All people of the earth have the same access to God through the true and living way that has been disclosed in Jesus Christ.

Paul, and the other writers of the New Testament, clearly give witness to the historical Jesus, the Christ, as the normative disclosure of God's salvation. However, they point to him as the historical focus of the light that has shone in the darkness from the beginning. The earthly Jesus does not represent the beginning of God's salvation. Rather, he is the historical climax of that salvation. He is the historical demonstration par excellence of God's eternal will and plan to rescue humankind from darkness. Thus the New Testament recognizes that although God has acted through Israel to reveal himself in a special way, his salvation has not been limited to those who through historical circumstance share in that tradition. Neither is it now so limited.

Finally, Paul and the other apostolic missioners focused their attention on basic human relationships rather than religious philosophies. They were concerned to transform those social and individual attitudes and patterns of behavior that disrupt and alienate human beings from each other. They warned against getting involved in academic controversies about religious philosophies (Col 2:8). Rather they urged respect, mutual helpfulness, kindness, compassion and integrity, and they leveled their criticism at those social-spiritual values and practices that were dehumanizing.

Of course, in this they were not alone. Among the pagans there were people of integrity who upheld such basic human values. Sin was not defined in terms of cultural or religious ideologies but in terms of selfish greed and disrespect for the "image of God" in fellow human beings. Thus they condemned such cultural practices as slavery, violence against the weak, sexual promiscuity, prostitution, pederasty, wife and child abuse, and idolatry. Idolatry, the last-mentioned item, has to do with superstitious delusion and the political and social domination of the "powers" that destroy the image of God. Idols thus represent the greedy wish projections of their makers.

Thus we observe that Paul attempted to introduce a transforming dynamic into the religious and cultural pluralism of the first-century world without pitting one religion against another. Since every human culture stands equally under the redeeming scrutiny of God, all are called to submit to the judgment and grace of God. This certainly is not an approach of cultural or religious imperialism. Paul self-consciously identified himself as a "servant" of Christ (Rom 1:1) and made his appeal in "weakness" (2 Cor 2:3). If this is imperialistic, it is an imperialism of the cross.

Theological Considerations

Many of our old mission rubrics were formulated when "crusading" Christianity was at its height. They have, in fact, become restrictive, like old wineskins that have lost their elasticity. We need to reexamine the fundamental theological definitions that carry the message of the cross and reformulate them so that they do not carry imperialistic implications. The cross is not an imperial instrument to be used in a crusade! Unlike a sword, which also is cruciform, the cross has no handle.

During this time of shifting cultural paradigms, many Christians are reexamining their understanding of the uniqueness of Christ. Some hold to an "exclusivist" position, based on traditional Protestant orthodoxy. These assert that salvation is exclusively through the historical manifestation of Jesus on the cross. The historical biblical tradition is considered a "special" or "supernatural" revelation that has saving power, while "general" or "natural" revelation can enlighten but not enable salvation.

Others take an "inclusivist" position, based on Catholic orthodoxy or a Protestant rereading of the biblical message. These hold that the historical disclosure in Jesus exhibits God's method of salvation through the eternal "Word" or "cosmic Christ." He is the "light" that from the beginning has been the life and light (salvation) of humankind. So while salvation comes only through the Christ, it is not limited to an explicit knowledge of the historical cross. However, the atoning grace made explicit in Christ remains the normative way of salvation.

A third, "pluralist" position understands the saving activity of God even more broadly. God is said to be at work in all religions. Thus all religions can be effective paths to salvation. Christ is normative for Christians, but not for Hindus, Buddhists or other cultural religious groups.

In light of this ongoing theological debate in missiology, we need to reexamine our basic theological definitions. While theological insight will not immediately dictate a strategy for dealing with persons of other religions, it can be most helpful in setting the direction, priorities and goals of our intervention strategies.

Some Theological Theses

First, we must examine the implications of the Christian view that *there is only one God, who is the loving God of all humankind.* This one God is the Creator-Savior of the human race from the beginning of time. God is not the Creator of the *whole* human race who genuinely offers salvation to only *part* of that race. That is the implication of the Augustinian concept of salvation of the elect only, which has permeated much of Christian orthodoxy.[2] To say this does not necessarily commit us to believe in a predetermined universal salvation, but it connotes that salvation is universally available through the gracious intervention of the one Creator-Savior God. He has not left himself without witness. Neither has he restricted himself to the historical witness of the church. Thus as we cross cultural and religious boundaries, we look for the signs of God's presence and self-revelation.

Furthermore, God did not begin to be Savior only with the coming of Jesus. Indeed, the creation story of Genesis is told as a salvation story. The earth in chaos and darkness is given light and fructifying order. Light and life are the biblical symbols for salvation. When the Gospel of John tells us that

Jesus brought light and life to the world, it identifies him as the embodiment of the life-giving Word effective in creation. This God, who is the source of all life, light and order from the beginning of the universe, is Savior of the world. Thus the Bible itself implies that God is at work from the beginning, before and outside the Abrahamic and Mosaic traditions, for the salvation of all humankind.

This one God has *revealed* himself universally for the life of all humankind. In fact, God's revelation, or self-disclosure, is equated with God's acts of creation and salvation. As the psalmist wrote, if God hides his face from us we die (Ps 104:29). God's revelation is a gracious self-communication, a giving of Godself for the life of the world. It is a creative and saving word that is the source of life and light. Thus we must attribute genuine salvific potential to the various channels of general revelation.

In Protestant orthodoxy, "special" revelation has been identified with "supernatural" revelation, and "general" with "natural." Natural revelation, it is held, is enough to make humans responsible for their sin, but it does not impart "saving grace." Supernatural grace is available only within the confines of special revelation. In this manner salvation is made the exclusive prerogative of the biblical disclosure culminating in Christ. This qualitative distinction between the effects of special (supernatural) and general (natural) revelation, which is implicit if not explicit in the exclusivist position, is biblically untenable.

Throughout the history of humankind God has spoken in "many and various ways" (Heb 1:2-3), and finally this "Word" was definitively embodied in the life and message of Jesus Christ (Jn 1:14).[3] Thus the light that shines in Jesus is identified with the universal light "which enlightens everyone, . . . coming into the world" (Jn 1:9). This is the biblical basis for the concept of the "cosmic Christ."

The cosmic Light and Word of God is not reduced to the historical Jesus, but rather Jesus is the historical embodiment of the cosmic self-disclosure. Thus John presents Jesus as "the light of the world," and he maintains that whoever is truly interested in "the light" will recognize Jesus (Jn 8:12). John does not claim that Jesus is "exclusively" the light, but that those who "love the light" will come to him (3:19-21). We need to reexamine the implications of this universal note in God's self-communication for our attitudes and approach to other religious traditions.

Second, we need to reexamine our concept of salvation. *Salvation is healing, not an instantaneous rescue from perdition.* Sōzō, the New Testament word for salvation, means to heal or rescue from a life-destroying condition. Social healing is described as reconciliation. Personal healing from shame and guilt is described as forgiveness and justification. Healing from ethical and spiritual disorders is called regeneration. But the root idea is healing. The purpose of salvation is a new life (joy), shalom (peace) and righteousness (justice), not religious rites and ideology (Rom 14:17).

Salvation is both a process (healing) and goal (health), and it applies to both individuals and societies. (Revelation 22:2 speaks of the healing of the nations.) Further, healing is a holistic concept. The goal of individual salvation is personal wholeness—spiritual, social and physical health. The goal of social salvation is shalom, or the peace of God, which includes material, social and spiritual well-being. Such holistic healing is indicated in the prayer "Your kingdom come."

If God is the Creator-Savior continuously involved in the life of the world, and salvation is the process of healing and being healed, then we can understand how our presence can be truly a working together with God to reconcile and rehabilitate the world. As followers of the light, Christians are to be present in the world as "salt" and "light" (Mt 5:13-16). It is significant that this expression follows a description of disciples as the righteous poor who long for justice and peace in the world.

Third, *salvation is by grace,* not by religion. No one is saved by religious practices such as going to church, offering sacrifices or making donations to temples. These are identified in Scripture as "works of the flesh." As Paul put it, "Neither circumcision nor uncircumcision is anything; but a new creation is everything!" (Gal 6:15). This certainly suggests that participation or nonparticipation in religious rites is not of the essence. Religions as such are not the bearers of salvation, not even the Christian religion. No matter in which religious culture one is socialized, one is saved only by the gracious God who is revealed in Jesus Christ.

In Romans 2 the apostle Paul makes this same point in the context of Judaism. He makes the point so emphatically that he pauses at the beginning of chapter 3 to ask the rhetorical question "Then what advantage has the Jew?" The answer for both cultural Jews and Christians is the same, namely, that they have the advantage of standing in the historical tradition from which Christ came (3:1-2). We must note, however, that this can also be a disadvantage when the tradition becomes perverted.

In Japan I was sometimes asked what would have been different if Jesus had been born in Japan. The answer, of course, is that the historical person Jesus the Christ was the product of a historical tradition, and it would have been impossible for him to be born in another tradition. He would simply have been another person. It is this inescapable historical limitation that gives moral force to the evangelical imperative.

The biblical formula of salvation "by grace through faith" has clear implications for our relation to people of other religions. "Through faith" indicates that cultural religious observances as such do not save us. However, such practices may be evidence of a sincere faith response to grace. One is reminded of the pagan father who pled with Jesus, "I believe; help my unbelief!" (Mt 9:24). Or of the words of Jesus that faith even the size of a mustard seed will be effective (Mt 17:20). Just as we distinguish between faith and our own imperfect religious response, so we must differentiate faith and works for others. Religious observance *may be* the response of sincere faith, and as such it may be an appeal to God's grace. Or it may be the assertion of human authority in an attempt to control one's own destiny.

Since grace is the preeminent manifestation of *agape,* to say that salvation is only by grace also means that the only way to life is the way of *agape* (love). Indeed, the very concept of *agape* is defined in the life, death and resurrection of Jesus, who gave himself for the life of the world. To put this negatively, there are not many different ways of salvation or many different saviors. But wherever we see such *agape* expressed, we recognize the countenance of saving grace.

By formal definition *agapē,* or *ḥesed* in the Hebrew, is God's relation to us described as his covenant law of "life and well-being" (Mal 2:5). Substantively, it is the kind of relation displayed in Jesus Christ and described by him as the "reign of God." The prayer "Your kingdom come; your will be done on earth as in heaven" is a prayer for the salvation of the world. This salvation from the human side is received through a positive response to the life, light and love (the

Word) that comes from God. Where we glimpse such agapaic relations and action, we may conclude that God's saving grace is present and at work.

Fourth, *religions are relative human responses to the light of God which has shone in human darkness.* Religions are cultural, human expressions. While they are responses to revelation, we should not speak of them as revealed. This is true of all religions, including Christianity. The old teaching that Christianity is a "revealed religion" and the others are "natural religions" gives us a false lead in relating to those of other religious faiths. The ritual, moral and theological response of the Christian church to God's revelation in Christ has been imperfect and relative, like those of other religions. We need to keep this in mind when we engage in comparative dialogue or attempt to give witness to Christ.

Unfortunately, the prevailing human response to revelation has been self-centered and negative—a phenomenon that theology refers to as "original sin." Indeed, as the apostle Paul looked at his religious world, both Jewish and pagan, he was very pessimistic about human response patterns (Rom 1:18-25). These negative responses, as well as the positive ones, have been institutionalized in the religions of the world. Thus while one must always deal sensitively and with respect in matters of religious conviction, one does not assume that a "religious" response is ipso facto a life-enhancing response. As the old spiritual suggests, there is "good religion" and "bad religion." Our concern for ourselves and others is to have good religion.

Whatever advantage Christianity may have does not derive from the religious response of Christianity, but only from the Christ. Thus we need to make a very clear distinction between revelation, biblical faith and Christianity as a cultural religious phenomenon. Revelation is the light and life-giving warmth of God as it radiates in the world. Faith is recognition of and positive response to that light. And for Christians, Jesus Christ is the normative expression of that light. Christianity as a theological ideology and system of religious rites and moral requirements varies greatly from culture to culture, and itself must be judged by its faithfulness to the new vision of the kingdom of God that Christ disclosed.

We must be very careful not to promote *our* religion in competition with *their* religion. The light is not the prerogative of any one religion. We can appeal only to a self-authenticating authority in life as Jesus himself did, not to religion. That authentication was the power of the Holy Spirit, which was manifest in and through his ministry for human well-being. And Jesus assured his disciples that this same Holy Spirit, the Paraclete, will give such authentication to their ministry (Jn 16:8-11).

Fifth, *when light is refused, it becomes exposure and judgment* (Jn 3:19-21). Such a negative response usually takes the form of psychological denial or, in theological terms, self-justification. Cultures have a bias for the authority of tradition, and the initial reaction is to give it precedence over the inbreaking light: "We are OK. This is our way. Nothing is wrong. You have no right to interfere with our culture."

The tobacco industry's reaction to findings about the effects of cigarette smoking is an excellent example of such denial. While its representatives argue vehemently that cigarettes are not deadly, and smokers insist on continuing, people keep dying from smoking ("judgment"). But those who listen and abstain or quit become healthier ("salvation").

The human predisposition to this kind of reaction should

caution us against naiveté in our relations to people of other faiths, and especially in our relations to any institutionalized system. We must be "wise as serpents and harmless as doves." At the same time this awareness should greatly humble us and open our eyes to the denial in our own culture. We must not try to clean the speck of dust from someone else's eye when we have a log in our own.

Finally, in our review of theological fundamentals, we need to face the question so often raised whether one can be "saved" without knowledge of the earthly Jesus. I am quite confident that from a biblical perspective the answer is yes. Here we must make a theological distinction between Jesus the historical person and the Christ or the Word, the active principle of God's self-disclosure. We have a good example of this distinction in 1 Corinthians 10:4, where Paul identifies the "spiritual rock" from which Israel drank in the wilderness with "Christ." And John, in a figurative utterance, represents Jesus as saying, "Before Abraham was, I am" (Jn 8:58). Obviously this "I am" does not mean the historical Jesus of Nazareth, born of Mary. All the "I am" sayings in the Gospel of John refer ultimately to "the Word" that "became flesh" in Jesus (1:14).

According to the biblical story, God has made covenants of salvation with humankind from the beginning of creation. *Adam* means humankind, and when it is used as the name for the father of the race it represents the whole human race. Noah represents a new beginning of the human race, and again God made a covenant with his family for the salvation of humanity. Then at a later date we read of Melchizedek, priest of the Most High God, whom Abraham recognized as God's priest. All of these characters represent humankind outside the Abrahamic tradition but, of course, not outside the scope of God's saving self-disclosure. None of them knew about the earthly Jesus or even worshiped Yahweh as God, yet all of them "pleased God" (Heb 11:5).

Abraham represents the beginning of the historical tradition that culminates in the coming of Jesus. Abraham became the prototype of "salvation by faith" because he anticipated the fulfillment of God's promised salvation. Jesus referred to this anticipatory faith as "seeing my day" (see Jn 8:56), but this does not mean that Abraham knew the earthly Jesus. It is significant that Paul makes Abraham the progenitor of the faithful, rather than Moses, the prophet of institutionalized Israelite religion. Abraham, the polygamous desert chieftain who glimpsed a God beyond the sun and moon but thought God wanted him to sacrifice his son Isaac on a distant mountain, is "father of the faithful."

One should note also that the prophets and apostles are not nearly so exclusive in their assessment of God's saving exploits as are many modern Christians. Amos challenged the Israelites' presumption that they were God's favorites (9:7). Jonah was called to warn the Ninevites and, to his own dismay, witnessed their salvation. Paul criticized the Jews for assuming that God's goodness meant God's exclusive approval and warned them that judgment would be according to deeds, not preferential standing (Rom 2:4-7). Peter was shown that "God shows no partiality" in his saving concern (Acts 10:34).

Thus we conclude that God is at work for the salvation of humankind in cultures and religions outside the confines of God's historical revelation to Israel. It is wrong to assume that no one in these cultures is "saved" until the story of Jesus is told. Indeed, one should go to these cultures with the presumption that God is already there and effectively at work, and that the message of Jesus will be self-authenticating when it is presented in deed and word.

Practical Considerations

People's religion is part of their cultural identity. Thus our relationships to individuals of other cultures and faiths inevitably involve us in relations with their cultures' religions. One cannot, for example, relate with integrity to individual Hindus in any depth without taking their Hindu religion seriously. To ignore their religious culture is to not take them seriously. To simply reject their religion as "heathen" or demonic inevitably means rejecting the people whose identity is bound up with it.

I remember how sensitive Indian Christians refused to sing the hymn "From Greenland's Icy Mountains to India's Coral Strands" because of the words "The heathen in their blindness bow down to wood and stone." While they did not necessarily agree with their Hindu friends, they deemed this to be a prejudiced judgment. A young Japanese woman studying at a Christian college in America asked me, "Do you think that Japanese people are bad?" When I inquired why she asked, she told me some classmates thought that Buddhism is a heathen (bad) religion.

Further, to reject a religious culture in toto as evil implies that individuals must leave it in order to follow Christ. When nineteenth-century missionaries presumed that heathen cultures with their religions were simply the work of the devil, they assumed that those cultures were incapable of becoming vehicles to carry the gospel. Converts were expected to reject their own culture and join the culture of the Western compound in order to be Christian. This implies, for example, that a self-sacrificing act of love by a committed Hindu cannot be an act of true *agape*. Or that such a Hindu's adoration of Christ as his or her Istadevi (own personal god) cannot be pleasing to God. This, of course, was Augustine's presumption, and it has remained the presumption of orthodoxy.

The principles of contextualization, or inculturation, of the gospel and a holistic approach to mission demand a revision of such assumptions. To contextualize means to communicate the gospel from within a given culture and in terms relevant to that culture. And if we are to be holistic, we must approach individuals in their culture and search for ways the gospel can be a catalyst for change, both in the life of individuals and in the society. Jesus did not require Jews to become non-Jews but rather to enter the kingdom in the context of their own religious culture.

Such a holistic approach to other cultures (religions) raises many issues, especially for those who assume a clear separation between religious faith and societal culture. Such people have thought of Christian faith in individualistic "spiritual" terms and have read many of their modern Western cultural biases into Scripture. They are often unaware of how much they have identified their own cultural expressions of scriptural values with the meaning and spirit of Scripture itself. They do not recognize to what extent their own identities are bound up with particular forms of moral and religious practice. But if we are to effectively relate our faith to people of other faiths, we must learn the fine art of crosscultural critique. Such critique requires an increasing self-awareness, a historical perspective on the biblical message and a reflective analysis of our own cultural religious forms.

While we want to avoid mere eclecticism and syncretism, we must open ourselves to the possibility that cultural practices foreign to us do convey meanings compatible with the gospel. This requires that we distinguish between the meanings we project onto other cultural forms and the inner meaning these practices have for people to whom the culture is native. It also requires us to learn what our cultural practices may convey to them.

We must ask again what faith in Christ implies across cultures and how it will be manifest in any and every culture. How will faith in Christ change human individuals within their respective cultures? What will it mean in a given culture to take up the cross and follow Jesus? What will it mean to be "crucified and buried with Christ" in order that they and we may experience the power of the resurrection?

The essential message of the cross and resurrection is that through the living Christ, God is among us as the power of *agape* to bring strength out of weakness, to seek reconciliation rather than vengeful justice, to destroy the barriers and walls of suspicion that create hostility and alienation among humans and between humankind and God. "For he [Christ] is our peace" (Eph 2:14).

When I was in India in 1966 I spent several days in Sevagram, the village where Mahatma Gandhi lived in the closing days of his life. I had opportunities to step inside Gandhi's home, which was being kept open as a memorial to his influence. On the side of the small living room where he sat on the floor to read and work were the cushions he had used. Directly across the room, just at eye level, was a familiar Western painting of Jesus Christ with the words "He is our Peace" below it.

About a decade later, my wife and I visited Sevagram, which had now become a museum. No one was living in the village. After showing my wife various other buildings, I led her into Gandhi's home to show her the motto of Christ, but it was gone. When I inquired about its absence, I was told that it had been moved to the museum in Delhi because some right-wing Hindus had objected to its presence, and the caretakers did not want to give offense.

To me this was a parable of the scandal of the Christian mission. Of course the Christ of the cross is, as Paul said, a "scandal." But compounded with this essential scandal of "weakness" and "foolishness" (1 Cor 1:21-25) was the scandal of an imperialistic mission in the name of this Christ of peace.

As I traveled over India I visited numerous Christian cathedrals that included memorials to British rulers and soldiers who had been there as representatives of Christ. This was what the right-wing, nationalistic Hindus were reacting against. From the Hindu side, Gandhi had been graced to see beyond the façade of Christendom to the Christ who is our peace, even though he did not claim to be Christian. It is our task from the Christian side to authentically represent this Christ in word and deed.

As crosscultural change agents, we are responsible to make explicit the distinction between our faith in Christ and Western religion. We need to remain aware of our own cultural identity and learn how to introduce Christ, not Western Christianity, so that he will influence others' way of life. The people of Asia and Africa assume that America is a "Christian culture." They assume that we as American Christians share the attitudes, values and politics of our national society. When we intervene with a hope for transformational change, the burden of proof otherwise is on us.

Finally, in all of this it is important to remember that we are dealing with people and not ideologies. Christian witness is not an argument to be won but an act of genuine caring for other people. Thus in all our relationships and decisions we must be flexible and concerned for the other person's welfare. We must be open and honest in our responses to them. We do not have all the answers, and our cultural religion is not always better in every way! An authentic witness to Christ will give the recipients freedom to consider how Jesus relates to them in their culture.

For the sake both of the community and the individual, care must be taken not to unnecessarily alienate individuals from their cultural settings. Both Jesus and Paul warn about the seriousness of unwarranted offenses (Mt 18:7; 1 Cor 10:32). On the other hand, we want to motivate and enable individuals and local groups to achieve their highest God-given destiny as it has been revealed in Christ. And as observed above, this may involve changes in cultural practices.

The line between alienation and transformational change is often tough to call. For example, in cultures where local customs denigrate women, how can we work for the humane changes implicit in the gospel? A call for such change inevitably implies criticism of the local tradition. Certainly in such situations relationships must be solidified through presence and respect before our criticism can be transformational. And it is precisely in such situations that we must appeal to a higher principle and authority than our own cultural example. We go not as representatives of Western Christianity, but of the Christ who judges and redeems both Christianity and every other religion by the same standard.

Notes

Introduction

[1]*Agapē* is the New Testament word indicating the kind of love that was demonstrated in the life of Jesus. In the Latin Bible it was translated *caritas,* hence "charity" in English ethical and theological treatises. I will be using *agape* and the adjective *agapaic* throughout the essay in its original New Testament sense to denote Christlike, compassionate love.

Chapter 1: Christian Witness in a Postmodern Context

[1]In their book *Mennonite Peacemaking: From Quietism to Activism* (Scottdale, Penn.: Herald, 1993), Leo Driedger and Donald Kraybill describe how certain forces of modernity have affected close-knit Mennonite communities. These same features have been present in and part of our intervention programs across cultures:

1. "Application of technology to virtually every dimension of life—from birth control to embalmment, from robotic production to genetic engineering" (p. 40).

2. A "rationalistic" and scientific approach that emphasizes management, control and choice—the parameters in "development."

3. "Individualization," which breaks down the sanctions of collective values and goals and stresses private individual rights and freedoms (democracy) and capitalistic economics (entrepreneurship).

4. "Differentiation"—the *specialization* of occupations and social functions, which erodes the cohesive community structures, and the *diversity* of ideas and values caused by new technologies of communication.

5. Secularization—a loss of the sense of the sacred mystery of life (the desacralization of culture), which undercuts the deep religious presuppositions and values that are the foundation of culture.

Driedger and Kraybill note that "specialization, mobility and technology in the modern world unravel the structural ties that knot the individual into long term relationships with permanent groups" (ibid., p. 42). Operating in the modern mode, we have too often furthered a process of cultural erosion that was actually inimical to the gospel!

[2]Howard Snyder's *Earth Currents: The Struggle for the World's Soul* (Nashville: Abingdon, 1995) explores the movement from a number of perspectives.

[3]See the little volume of essays edited by Frederic Burnham, *Postmodern Theology: Christian Faith in a Pluralist World* (San Francisco: Harper, 1989). The essays by James Miller and Sandra Schneiders will be especially helpful in marking out the significant changes for Christian faith.

[4]See David Lockhead, *The Dialogical Imperative: A Christian Reflection on Interfaith Encounter* (Maryknoll, N.Y.: Orbis, 1988), for an excellent treatment of this point. Lockhead points out that dialogue is a relationship that the Bible speaks of as *agapē.*

[5]See Hiebert's article "Critical Contextualization," *Missiology* 12, no. 3 (July 1984): 287-96.

[6]In his autobiography as told to Joseph Shenk, Kisare, an African bishop, explains how a serious offender who had been excluded from the village could be reconciled only after a blood sacrifice had been offered. See *Kisare, a Mennonite of Kiseru* (Salunga, Penn.: Eastern Mennonite Board of Missions, 1984), p. 79.

[7]C. Norman Kraus, *The Authentic Witness: Credibility and Authority* (Grand Rapids, Mich.: Eerdmans, 1979), p. 45.

[8]In the early 1970s Elton Trueblood wrote a perceptive defense of the intercultural Christian mission, which for him includes both evangelism and social service. Already at that time relativistic pluralism was rejecting the right of Christianity to press its faith claims on other cultures. Trueblood argued that "the faith of Christ . . . conforms to reality as does no other alternative of which we are aware" and that these claims can be substantiated in empirical experience. (See chap. 3 in D. Elton Trueblood, *The Validity of the Christian Mission* [New York: Harper & Row, 1972].)

[9]Kristen A. Grace, D. Merrill Ewert and Paul R. Eberts, "MCCers and Evangelicals: Perspectives of Development," *Conrad Grebel Review,* Fall 1995, pp. 365-84.

[10]Paul Hiebert and Barbara Hiebert-Crape, "The Role of Religion in International Development," *Conrad Grebel Review,* Fall 1995, p. 291.

[11]John Driver, "The Anabaptist Vision and Social Justice," in *Freedom and Discipleship,* ed. Daniel Schipani (Maryknoll, N.Y.: Orbis, 1989), p. 109.

Chapter 2: Intervention

[1]In his contribution to the Evangelism and Social Responsibility conference (Wheaton College, 1983), Wayne Bragg offered a "transformation" model to go "beyond development." This language was first used by evangelicals to indicate the need for a more radical spiritual approach to the relief and development work of the churches. In his *Getting to the Twenty-first Century: Voluntary Action and the Global Agenda* (Hartford, Conn.: Kumarian, 1990) David Korten adopts the language without its evangelical implications.

[2]For a description of what such a community involves see my *Community of the Spirit: How the Church Is in the World,* rev. ed. (Scottdale, Penn.: Herald, 1993).

[3]See Korten, *Getting to the Twenty-first Century.*

[4]I owe these insights into the limitations of the metaphor to Wayne Teel, who is currently an assistant professor at Eastern Mennonite University.

[5]See David Lockhead, *The Dialogical Imperative: A Christian Reflection on Interfaith Encounter* (Maryknoll, N.Y.: Orbis, 1988).

[6]I emphasize this because so much of the language of pluralism and relativism implies a presence or dialogue that ends in tolerance of the status quo. The outcome is merely appreciation of and respect for each other's relative values as the only necessary change.

[7]See Calvin Shenk's helpful pamphlet entitled *A Relevant Theology of Presence* (Elkhart, Ind.: Mission Focus, 1982).

[8]For example, see Sandra Franklin and Melody Rupley, "Presence Versus Intervention," *MCC Intercom,* February 1993.

Chapter 3: Reorienting the Conceptual Framework for Mission

[1]See *Thoughts on Development,* rev. ed., in the Mennonite Economic Development Associates Monograph Series, 1975-, Mennonite Central Committee. The series contains a number of essays relating development to its various aspects—

education, family life, health and so on.

[2]David Korten, *Getting to the Twenty-first Century: Voluntary Action and the Global Agenda* (Hartford, Conn.: Kumarian, 1990); quotes are from pp. 168, xiii and again 168.

[3]David Wright, "The Pitfalls of the International Aid Rationale: Comparisons Between Missionary Aid and the International Aid Network," *Missiology* 2, no. 2 (1994).

[4]Already in 1947 Carl F. H. Henry called attention to *The Uneasy Conscience of Modern Fundamentalism* (Grand Rapids, Mich.: Eerdmans). In the fifty years since then we have seen some movement toward a more holistic mission, but the gap between academic missiology and actual practice in the evangelical world is disheartening. The contemporary journal *Transformation*, edited by a panel of international evangelical scholars, continues to work at this hiatus.

[5]See Gordon Aeschliman, "Outside the Gate," *Sojourners*, May-June, 1995, pp. 22-26. For a fuller analysis of the character of evangelical action see also my article "Evangelicalism: A Mennonite Critique," in *The Variety of American Evangelicalism*, ed. Donald Dayton and Robert K. Johnston (Downers Grove, Ill.: InterVarsity Press, 1991), pp. 184-203.

[6]In his famous sermon "The New Being," Paul Tillich captured the dynamic of Paul's vision. "We want only to show you something we have seen and to tell you something we have heard: That in the midst of the old creation there is a New Creation, and that this New Creation is manifest in Jesus who is called the Christ" (*The New Being* [New York: Scribner's, 1955], p. 18).

[7]Very early in the Christian tradition even the saving ministry of Jesus was interpreted as a *deus ex machina*, that is, not as a full human embodiment identifying with us but as an imperial visitation exercising supernatural powers. The apocryphal Gospels are full of magical exploits of the infant and child Jesus rescuing from danger, providing food, punishing evil deeds and the like.

[8]Louis Luzbetak, *The Church and Cultures* (Maryknoll, N.Y.: Orbis, 1988), pp. 168, 161.

Chapter 4: What Kind of Intervention?

[1]For example, we do not have an adequate theology of the spirituality of work. Miroslav Volf, an evangelical from Croatia now teaching at Fuller Theological Seminary, speaks of the "materiality of salvation" and "God's desire to bring integrity to the whole human being including the body, and to the whole of injured reality" (*Work in the Spirit: Toward a Theology of Work* [New York: Oxford University Press, 1991], p. 104).

[2]It is not my purpose to critique capitalism as an economic system, but while the Christian Scriptures presume private ownership, they do not endorse the profit motive as the sole guiding dynamic for economic activity. Paul's word is that accumulation of wealth is for the purpose of sharing with those in need (Eph 4:28). In *The Clashing Worlds of Economics and Faith* (Scottdale, Penn.: Herald, 1995), James Halteman has written a persuasive critique of the inherent tensions between capitalistic economics and Christian faith.

[3]David Korten, *Getting to the Twenty-first Century: Voluntary Action and the Global Agenda* (Hartford, Conn.: Kumarian, 1990), p. 168.

[4]I discuss the question of our relation as Christians to people of other faiths in chapter seven.

[5]I might add here that I think it is necessary to give an explicit witness to Christ in our intervention ministries for two reasons. First, we need to disassociate ourselves from Western Christianity as a cultural religion. This is especially true in Asia. Second, we need to identify the source and enabling power for the new possibilities and patterns we offer. We are not offering a cultural religious presence and remedial package! But more of this later.

[6]Louis Luzbetak, *The Church and Cultures* (Maryknoll, N.Y.: Orbis, 1988), p. 314.

[7]Walter Wink, *Naming the Powers: The Language of Power in the New Testament* (Minneapolis: Fortress, 1984), p. 117.

[8]Terry Alliband, *Catalysts of Development: Voluntary Agencies in India* (West Hartford, Conn.: Kumarian, 1983), pp. 102-3; the emphasis is mine.

[9]Dor Bahadur Bista, *Fatalism and Development: Nepal's Struggle for Modernization* (Calcutta: Orient Longman, 1991).

[10]See pt. 1 of Walter Wink's *Engaging the Powers: Discernment and Resistance in a World of Domination* (Minneapolis: Fortress, 1992).

[11]For Paul even sanctification is not exclusively a theological concept. He prays that the Thessalonians might be sanctified in "spirit and soul [reason] and body" (1 Thess 5:23), which suggests a physical aspect of holiness. The first two commandments, which summarize them all, include loving both God and our fellow humans. To do God's will on earth is to "do justice, and to love kindness, and to walk humbly with . . . God" (Mic 6:8). This is echoed in James 1:27 (my paraphrase): "Religion that is pure and undefiled before God is this: to care for orphans and widows in their distress and to keep oneself unco-opted by this world."

Chapter 5: A Christian Spirituality for Intervention Ministries

[1]Walter Wink, *Naming the Powers: The Language of Power in the New Testament* (Minneapolis: Fortress, 1984), p. 117.

[2]Lynn Samaan, "Spiritual Formation for Relief and Development Workers," in *Christian Relief and Development: Developing Workers for Effective Ministry,* ed. Edgar J. Elliston (Dallas: Word, 1989), p. 133.

[3]Following in the tradition of Elton Trueblood, Richard Foster has written about spirituality as a discipline of the inner life (*Celebration of Discipline: The Path to Spiritual Growth* [San Francisco: Harper & Row, 1978]). And David Bosch, the South African missiologist, wrote of a practical spirituality for missionaries in *A Spirituality of the Road* (Scottdale, Penn.: Herald, 1979).

[4]Barbara Hendricks and Thomas Clarke, "Spiritual Formation for Mission," in *Toward the Twenty-first Century in Christian Mission,* ed. James M. Phillips and Robert T. Coote (Grand Rapids, Mich.: Eerdmans, 1993), p. 204.

[5]*Confession of Faith in a Mennonite Perspective* (adopted in 1995), article 18.

[6]Aloysius Pieris, *Love Meets Wisdom: A Christian Experience of Buddhism* (Maryknoll, N.Y.: Orbis, 1988).

[7]See Russell E. Richey and Donald G. Jones, eds., *American Civil Religion* (New York: Harper & Row, 1974), pp. 21-22. This article was first published in *Daedalus,* Winter 1967.

[8]Walter Wink, *Engaging the Powers: Discernment and Resistance in a World of Domination* (Minneapolis: Fortress, 1992), p. 191.

[9]Hendricks and Clarke, "Spiritual Formation for Mission," p. 211.

[10]Bosch, *Spirituality of the Road,* p. 37.

[11]Kosuke Koyama, *Waterbuffalo Theology* (Maryknoll, N.Y.: Orbis, 1974).

[12]Lynn Samaan defines spiritual formation as "1) Knowing and experiencing God in an intimate relationship, 2) holistic development towards holiness and Christ-likeness, and 3) obeying God and doing the work of his kingdom." This, she says, divides spiritual formation into the "knowing-being-doing components which are so vitally important to any learning or growing process" ("Spiritual Formation," p. 131). Samaan emphasizes that our real values (spirituality) shine through our actions and attitudes.

[13]Hendricks and Clarke, "Spiritual Formation for Mission," p. 204.

[14]Michael Collins Reilly, *Spirituality for Mission* (Maryknoll, N.Y.: Orbis, 1978), pp. 237-38.

[15]Samaan, "Spiritual Formation," p. 140.

[16]Bosch, *Spirituality of the Road,* pp. 32-33.

Chapter 6: Conversion and Social Transformation

[1]Charles Elliott, *Comfortable Compassion? Poverty, Power and the Church* (New York: Paulist, 1987).

[2]Walter Wink, *Engaging the Powers: Discernment and Resistance in a World of Domination* (Minneapolis: Fortress, 1992), p. 57.

[3]Ibid., pp. 101-2.

[4]Elliott, *Comfortable Compassion?* pp. 116-17.

[5]Wink, *Engaging the Powers,* p. 75.

[6]Václav Havel, *Living in Truth: Twenty-two Essays,* ed. Jan Vladislav (Boston: Faber & Faber, 1989), p. 91.

[7]Elliott, *Comfortable Compassion?* pp. 117-18. Compare Donald Kraybill's *The Upside-Down Kingdom,* rev. ed. (Scottdale, Penn.: Herald, 1990). In his prize-winning book sociologist Kraybill analyzes the nature of the sociopolitical kingdom Jesus proclaimed.

[8]Gustavo Guitiérrez, quoted in Wayne Bragg, "Beyond Development," in *The Church in Response to Human Need,* ed. Tom Sine (Monrovia, Calif.: MARC, 1983), p. 81.

[9]Bragg, "Beyond Development," pp. 71-82.

[10]See the Peru "Declaration Towards a Holistic Transformation in Latin America," *Mission Focus* 17, no. 1 (March 1989): 15.

[11]Lisa Hobbs, *India, India* (New York: McGraw-Hill, 1967), pp. 198-200.

[12]Harold Bender's "The Anabaptist Vision" was first presented as the presidential address at the American Society of Church History (1943). It has since been reprinted in many places and is available as a paperback booklet from Herald Press (Scottdale, Penn.).

[13]John R. Burkholder and Howard John Loewen have pointed out that there has been a major transition in the Mennonite understanding of the implications of our peace position. Mennonites have moved from a stance of "withdrawal," in which peace was understood in a rather passive mode, to a stance of "transformation," in which peace is understood in dynamic terms as both a transformational strategy and a goal. See John R. Burkholder, *Mennonites in Ecumenical Dialogue on Peace and Justice,* MCC Occasional Paper 7 (Akron, Penn.: Mennonite Central Committee, 1988), and Howard John Loewen, "Peace in the Mennonite Tradition," in *Baptism, Peace and the State in the Reformed and Mennonite Traditions,* ed. Ross T. Bender and Alan P. F. Sell (Waterloo, Ont.: Wilfrid Laurier University Press, 1991).

Chapter 7: Relating to People of Other Faiths

[1]Paul Tillich wrote, "It means that no religion as such produces the New Being. Circumcision is a religious rite, observed by the Jews; sacrifices are religious rites, observed by the pagans; baptism is a religious rite, observed by the Christians. All these rites do not matter—only a New Creation. And since these rites stand, in the words of Paul, for the whole religion to which they belong, we can say: No religion matters—only a new state of things" (*The New Being* [New York: Scribner's, 1955], p. 16).

[2]During the latter part of the seventeenth century, climaxing in the Synod of Dort (1618-1619), the Reformed churches' position hardened on the subject of "double predestination." Anabaptism had from the beginning maintained a position nearer to the Catholic doctrine on free will. Undoubtedly aware of the Reformed controversy, Peter Jansz Twisck, a Frisian Anabaptist, and his colleagues published a confession in which they explicitly rejected the implications of "double predestination." The atonement through Christ is universal, and God's condemnation results only from the *voluntary* rejection of it. Further, they rejected "the belief of those who say that Almighty God has indeed caused the word of reconciliation to be preached to all, or many, but does nevertheless withhold His grace from many of them, so that the greater part of mankind cannot accept the word of reconciliation and be saved." See articles 9-10 of "Confession of Faith, According to the Holy Word of God" (1617) in *Martyrs Mirror* (Scottdale, Penn.: Mennonite Publishing House, 1950), pp. 379-81. The Cornelis Ris Confession of 1766 makes the same points.

[3]The complete phrase in Hebrews 1:1 is "many and various ways through the prophets." The general purpose of the book is to compare Jesus with the revelation given through the Mosaic law and the Hebrew prophets. However, if we include the "prophet" who wrote Genesis, we must extend the concept of covenantal revelation back to creation, as the Genesis account does. It is on these grounds that I take the liberty of applying the text to all covenantal or salvific revelation.

For Further Reading

Alliband, Terry. *Catalysts of Development: Voluntary Agencies in India.* West Hartford, Conn.: Kumarian, 1983.

Amin, Samir. *Maldevelopment: Anatomy of a Global Failure.* Atlantic Highlands, N.J.: Zed, 1990.

Arias, Mortimer. "My Pilgrimage in Mission," *International Bulletin of Missionary Research,* January 1992, pp. 28-32.

Bender, Harold S. *The Anabaptist Vision.* Scottdale, Penn.: Herald, 1944.

Bista, Dor Bahadur. *Fatalism and Development: Nepal's Struggle for Modernization.* Calcutta: Orient Longman, 1991.

Black, Jan Knippers. *Development in Theory and Practice.* Boulder, Colo.: Westview, 1991.

Blomstrom, Magnus, and Bjorn Hettne. *Development Theory in Transition.* London: Zed, 1984.

Borg, Marcus. *Jesus: A New Vision.* New York: Harper, 1984. (See also Borg's *Conflict, Holiness and Politics in the Teaching of Jesus* [Lewiston, N.Y.: Edwin Mellen, 1984].)

Bosch, David J. *A Spirituality of the Road.* Scottdale, Penn.: Herald, 1979.

Burnham, Frederic B., ed. *Postmodern Theology: Christian Faith in a Pluralist World.* San Francisco: Harper, 1989.

Cadorette, Curt, ed. *Liberation Theology: An Introductory Reader.* Maryknoll, N.Y.: Orbis, 1992.

Chambers, Robert. *Poverty and Livelihoods: Whose Reality Counts?* Discussion Paper 347. Brighton, England: Institute of Development Studies, 1995.

Clarke, Thomas E., ed. *Above Every Name: The Lordship of Christ and Social Systems.* New York: Paulist, 1980.

Cook, William. "Spirituality in the Struggles for Social Justice: A Brief Latin American Anthology." *Missiology* 12, no. 2 (April 1984): 223-32.

Copeland, Warren R. *And the Poor Get Welfare: The Ethics of Poverty in the United States.* Nashville: Abingdon, 1994.

Corwin, Charles. "That There May Be Equality And Self-Sufficiency: Toward an Evangelical Theology of Development." *Missiology* 12, no. 3 (July 1984): 339-53.

Detweiler, Richard, and Calvin Shenk. *Theology of Presence: Implications for Mission.* Elkhart, Ind.: Mission Focus, 1986.

Driedger, Leo, and Donald B. Kraybill. *Mennonite Peacemaking: From Quietism to Activism.* Scottdale, Penn.: Herald, 1993.

Dupuis, Jacques. *Jesus Christ at the Encounter of World Religions.* Maryknoll, N.Y.: Orbis, 1991.

Elliott, Charles. *Comfortable Compassion? Poverty, Power and the Church.* New York: Paulist, 1987.

Elliston, Edgar J., ed. *Christian Relief and Development: Developing Workers for Effective Ministry.* Dallas: Word, 1989.

Fabella, Virginia, and Sun Ai Lee Park, eds. *We Dare to Dream: Doing Theology as Asian Women.* Maryknoll, N.Y.: Orbis, 1989.

Fackre, Gabriel, Ronald Nash and John Sanders. *What About Those Who Have Never Heard?* Downers Grove, Ill.: InterVarsity Press, 1995.

Foster, Richard J. *Celebration of Discipline: The Path to Spiritual Growth.* San Francisco: Harper & Row, 1978.

Griffiths, Paul J., ed. *Christianity Through Non-Christian Eyes.* Faith Meets Faith Series. Maryknoll, N.Y.: Orbis, 1990.

Goulet, Denis. *The Uncertain Promise: Value Conflicts in Technology Transfer.* New York: New Horizons, 1989.

Halteman, James. *The Clashing Worlds of Economics and Faith.* Scottdale, Penn.: Herald, 1995.

Hellwig, Monika K. "Good News to the Poor: Do They Understand It Better?" in *Tracing the Spirit: Communities, Social Action and Theological Reflection.* Edited by James E. Hug. New York: Paulist, 1983.

Henry, Carl F. H. *The Uneasy Conscience of Modern Fundamentalism.* Grand Rapids, Mich.: Eerdmans, 1947.

Korten, David C. *Getting to the Twenty-first Century: Voluntary Action and the Global Agenda.* Hartford, Conn.: Kumarian, 1990.

Koyama, Kosuke. *Three Mile an Hour God.* Maryknoll, N.Y.: Orbis, 1980.

———. *Waterbuffalo Theology.* Maryknoll, N.Y.: Orbis, 1974.

Kraus, C. Norman. *The Authentic Witness: Credibility and Authority.* Grand Rapids, Mich.: Eerdmans, 1979.

———. *The Community of the Spirit: How the Church Is in the World.* Rev. ed. Scottdale, Penn.: Herald, 1993.

Kraybill, Donald B. *The Upside-Down Kingdom.* Rev. ed. Scottdale, Penn.: Herald, 1990.

Kroeker, Peter J. "Development and Mission." *Mission Focus,* June 1987.

Lockhead, David. *The Dialogical Imperative: A Christian Reflection on Interfaith Encounter.* Maryknoll, N.Y.: Orbis, 1988.

Luzbetak, Louis J. *The Church and Cultures: New Perspectives in Missiological Anthropology.* Maryknoll, N.Y.: Orbis, 1988.

Oduyoye, Mercy Amba. *Hearing and Knowing: Theological Reflections on Christianity in Africa.* Maryknoll, N.Y.: Orbis, 1986.

Phillips, James M., and Robert T. Coote, eds. *Toward the Twenty-first Century in Christian Mission.* Grand Rapids: Eerdmans, 1993.

Reilly, Michael Collins. *Spirituality for Mission.* Maryknoll, N.Y.: Orbis, 1978.

Richey, Russell E., and Donald G. Jones, eds. *American Civil Religion.* New York: Harper & Row, 1974.

Sachs, Wolfgang. *On the Archaeology of the Development Idea.* University Park: Pennsylvania State University Press, 1989.

Shenk, Calvin. *A Relevant Theology of Presence.* Elkhart, Ind.: Mission Focus, 1982.

Shenk, David W. *Global Gods: Exploring the Role of Religions in Modern Societies.* Scottdale, Penn.: Herald, 1995.

Shenk, Wilbert R., ed. *The Transfiguration of Mission: Biblical, Theological and Historical Foundations.* Scottdale, Penn.: Herald, 1993.

Sine, Tom, ed. *The Church in Response to Human Need.* Monrovia, Calif.: MARC, 1983.

Snyder, Howard A. *Earth Currents: The Struggle for the World's Soul.* Nashville: Abingdon, 1995.

Stassen, Glen H. *Just Peacemaking: Transforming Initiatives for Justice and Peace.* Louisville, Ky.: Westminster John Knox, 1992.

Stoesz, Edgar. *Thoughts on Development.* MEDA Development Monograph Series 1. Akron, Penn.: Mennonite Central Committee, 1977.

Thomsen, Mark W. *The Word and the Way of the Cross: Christian Witness Among Muslim and Buddhist People.* Chicago: Evangelical Lutheran Church in America, Division for Global Ministry, 1993.

Trueblood, D. Elton. *The Validity of the Christian Mission.* New York: Harper & Row, 1972.

Vallely, Paul. *Bad Samaritans: First World Ethics and Third World Debt.* Maryknoll, N.Y.: Orbis, 1990.

Volf, Miroslav. *Work in the Spirit: Toward a Theology of Work.* New York: Oxford University Press, 1991.

Wallis, Jim. "Conversion—for the Sake of the World." Interview by Leon Howell. *International Review of Missions,* 1983, pp. 365-72. (The entire volume is on conversion.)

Weber, Joseph. "Christ's Victory over the Powers." In *Above Every Name: The Lordship of Christ and Social Systems,* pp. 66-82. Edited by Thomas Clarke. New York: Paulist, 1980.

Wink, Walter. *Engaging the Powers: Discernment and Resistance in a World of Domination.* Minneapolis: Fortress, 1992.

———. *Naming the Powers: The Language of Power in the New Testament.* Minneapolis: Fortress, 1984.

Wright, David. "The Pitfalls of the International Aid Rationale: Comparisons Between Missionary Aid and the International Aid Network." *Missiology* 22, no. 2 (1994): 187ff.